NAPA VALLEY

NAPA VALLEY

the Ultimate Winery Guide

REVISED AND UPDATED, THIRD EDITION

BY ANTONIA ALLEGRA

PHOTOGRAPHS BY RICHARD GILLETTE

FOREWORD BY ROBERT MONDAVI

CHRONICLE BOOKS

SAN FRANCISCO

Library of Congress Cataloging-in-Publication Data available.

ISBN 0-8118-2858-1

Printed in China.

Book design by Lisa Levin.
Cover design by Brett MacFadden.

Distributed in Canada by Raincoast Books
9050 Shaughnessy Street
Vancouver, British Columbia V6P 6E5

10 9 8 7 6 5 4 3 2 1

Chronicle Books LLC
85 Second Street
San Francisco, California 94105

www.chroniclebooks.com

DEDICATION

෧

For Donn, John, Deanna, Paul, Cathy, Madeline, Alex,

Jenny, Marty, Ethan, Alex B., and all my

family and friends who gather at the Treehouse

—Antonia

For my daughters Jasara and Holly and

grandson Zachary Martin, Sandra McMahon,

Dan and Bonnie Borghi, Shanti Finnerty,

Chuck and Camille Hathaway,

and the rest of my Mendocino family

—Richard

Without their inspiration, support, laughter,

and love, this book would not exist.

ACKNOWLEDGMENTS

We extend special thanks to these people who

went out of their way to help us create this book:

Maynard Amerine, Maria Lorraine Binchet,

Michael Carabetta, Martha Casselman,

Carey Charlesworth, Mary Frances Kennedy Fisher,

Jim Frisinger, Phil Hiaring of Wines and Vines,

Kelly Johnson, Leslie Jonath, Bill LeBlond,

Lisa Levin, Stephanie Rosenbaum, Ellen Russell,

Bill Ryan, Bob Steinhauer, John and Gladys Wichels,

and, especially, Harvey Posert.

CONTENTS

FOREWORD

Welcome to our lovely Napa Valley and to all its wineries! Whether you journey on Highway 29 or the Silverado Trail or take the armchair route through the pages of this book, you'll find numerous older wineries and many new ones eager to show you our renowned hospitality. Through the winery tours and your visits in our towns and restaurants, your enjoyment of wine will grow as you learn more about this land and its wonderful people. ✑ Each winery has its own point of view about grape growing and wine making—that's what makes wine so interesting. As you visit the individual wineries, ask about special programs on wine making, on the arts, and on wine and food. We all want to play a part in forming your happy memories of this valley. ✑ Bringing wine together with the arts and culture has been a special focus of my career. Even though ours is one of the newer wineries—it was the first winery built after Prohibition, in 1966—we join in a long tradition of wine and gastronomy as well as the fine arts: music, painting, sculpture, theater, and writing, and, here especially, architecture. ✑ Wine is the natural beverage for every celebration: the birth of a child, graduation, engagements, weddings, anniversaries, promotions, family gatherings, toasts between governments, and many other occasions. Wine can stand the scrutiny of any responsible citizen, because its benefits have been recognized for more than seven thousand years . . . since civilization began. And common sense tells us that wine will be with us forever as an integral part of our culture, heritage, and gracious way of life. ✑ I always knew that Napa Valley had the soils, climate, grape varieties, and people to make wines that rank on a par with the finest wines of the world. Fortunately, we have in the past decade been able to show connoisseurs in the Old and New Worlds that this is so; and we hope that you will share our enthusiasm, success, and enjoyment.

I raise a glass to the many guests who will enjoy this book and to their visits in the Napa Valley.

"To your health!"

Robert Mondavi

The play of color against the thirty-mile symmetry of neat vineyards bonds visitors and residents to this Napa Valley. ⁊ As you drive along the two north-south thoroughfares, the gentle mountain ranges act as backdrop to spectacular views, dappled with vineyard colors that depend on the time of year—the bright yellow of mustard plants at the feet of dormant vines in spring; a rich, verdant carpet of summer's grape leaves; the autumn olive, rust, burgundy, and sienna of a Renaissance tapestry; and finally the somber black and brown tones of winter. Sometimes, seen from an auto at fifty miles per hour, trellis wires give the impression of sheets of silver. The quality of light in this region is often extraordinary and has been the inspiration for many an artist's eye. ⁊ If your eye grabs a point and moves with it, you will see a blur of color. But allow the view to skip from row to row of vines and it will seem to be a series of mirrors, channels reflecting plants in various stages of life. In fact, it is the constant awareness of the life-growth-harvest cycle of renewal that invokes reflectiveness throughout the year. ⁊ The Napa Valley has been an agricultural hub since well before the Civil War. This was originally home to the Wappo and other tribes of Native Americans. Then, under General Mariano Vallejo, the area became Mexican California until the Bear Flag Republic revolt. In those early years, wheat, apples, prunes, walnuts, and a few grapevines were planted in the rocky soil. With the Victorian boom and the rise in popularity of locally made wines, the region flourished socially as well as agriculturally. The Prohibition years (1919–1933) closed most wineries and halted local development, but the valley has thrived since the mid-1960s and is again a popular visitors' spot. It has been named the third most popular natural tourist attraction in the state of California, following San Francisco and Yosemite. ⁊ Napa, Yountville, Oakville, Rutherford, St. Helena, and Calistoga dot the thirty-mile-long, five-mile-wide string of towns and cities along Highway 29 and the Silverado Trail. They act as centers for the locals and lodging, dining, and shopping places for visitors. But most of the valley's activity happens in the fields. ᏬᎧ Ninety percent of this valley is dedicated to agricultural use, and unlike neighboring Sonoma County, most of the earth on this side of the Mayacamas Range is planted to vines. Hillsides or meadows of cattle, horses, sheep, or goats are rare here. At seventy to one hundred thousand dollars a "valley floor acre" planted to Cabernet or Chardonnay, the land is too expensive for any cultivation other than grapes. As a result, this is an American wine-lover's paradise. ᏬᎧ Those who have visited the wine regions of Europe will see similarities in the rocky grape-growing terrains and occasionally in the vistas. However, I believe that there is one major difference from the tourist's point of view: in Europe, a vineyard visit is just that, a walk in the vineyard, if you're lucky. More often, it is a descent into a cool basement to taste some wine and make a purchase. If you wish to see imposing architecture accessible to the public, you must travel to the various chateaux regions that often are near but separated from the vineyards. And they often require special reservations. ᏬᎧ Here in the Napa Valley, a visitor has the best of all worlds. Superb wines are available at any of more than two hundred fifty wineries, and often the establishments are housed in magnificent structures themselves worthy of castle-visits. As it turns out, winery owners are the royalty of the Napa Valley, their kingdoms being vineyards and wineries. ᏬᎧ Perhaps this valley is so loved because it offers a magical sense of familiarity. For instance, this could easily be the setting for Jack and the Beanstalk's Happy Valley of fairy-tale lore. And millions viewed these hills and vineyards weekly during the screening of the *Falcon Crest* television series. But even more, being here feels like a homecoming to the best of rural America's simple life. ᏬᎧ In my hometown of St. Helena, certain daily observations still strike me as gifts rather than facts of life. I have lived in big cities and nothing there offers such basic pleasure as the morning greeting from the postman when I pick up my mail or the sound of frogs croaking on starry spring nights. The OK Barber Shop on Main Street hasn't changed its interior in at least fifty years, and its dull green, ecru, and chrome fixtures aren't likely to switch to those of a styling salon. Crusty country loaves continue to exit hot from the Model Baker's brick oven, and the town merchants chatter in the morning light as they sweep their sidewalk footage. Crime decreased by 31 percent in 1989 in St. Helena; there wasn't much to speak of before and hasn't been since. And a call-to-alarm alerts volunteer Fire Department members and townspeople of some strain in the otherwise calm life of the town. ✑ There are other images, too. There's a freckled boy—maybe ten years old—who frequently bicycles to school, tugging his laughing pal on a skateboard tied to the end of a rope. There is a sweet down-home honesty about this place. ✑ Ever-present birds add their joyful touch to daily life. Occasionally a flock of red-winged blackbirds will swoop to a fence rail, exposing a sudden surprise of brilliant red feathers at their shoulders. Or, when unpicked grapes still hang like udders from vines in December, it's not unusual for the sky to be filled with careening, twittering starlings, drunk from the yeasty vineyard fruit. ✑ Many Napa Valley residents grow grapes instead of lawn. With the drought of the 1980s and 1990s, a vineyard became more practical, requiring no mowing, and yielding wine grapes, which could be sold or pressed into wine. In fact, the residents can "drink their lawn." ✑ Where else in America would you see a "No Winery This Lane" sign along the highway? Or find almost three pages of winery listings in the telephone book? ✑ Often, with more than two hundred wineries on a valley list, it can be difficult to choose which to visit. And friends have told me, "We can't go wrong tasting Napa Valley wines, but we want to visit Victorian homes, too." To guide their preferences, I developed a personal annotated list for family and friends. Wineries with art collections. Spectacular gardens. Technical tours. Once on a serious path, I toured and screened wineries in the valley that are open to visitors. The wineries had to offer tours and be easily accessible, interesting, and visitor-friendly. To write this book, I finally identified the twenty-nine wineries that I believe fascinate and entertain visitors most with the Napa Valley wine-making art and way of life. My list is by no means meant to limit you in your travels in the Napa Valley. All the wineries here are marvelous, each with a different story and beauty. ❧ In all cases, I took standard tours. I did not seek or accept any gifts. The wineries chosen are here because they go out of their way to make visiting an educational and sensual pleasure. These are the wineries I suggest to my friends. ❧ I do not wish to overlook the multiple ways to view the Napa Valley. By air, there are hot air balloons, gliders, and biplanes. You can travel by bicycle or by horse or by train, or you can hike. And the possibilities for outstanding meals here are legendary. ❧ No matter how you visit here, no matter whether you stay at a resort, a hotel, a bed and breakfast inn, or in your friend's guest room, expect daily brushes with beauty mixed with the reality of the vineyard year. The combination may catch you unawares. Though this splendid valley of vines and winery "castles" may seem small, its greatness will be evident—in its people and in its wines.

Antonia Allegra
St. Helena, California

TOP 50 WINERIES TO VISIT IN THE NAPA VALLEY

1. S. Anderson Vineyards
2. Atlas Peak Vineyards
3. Artesa Winery *
4. Beaulieu Vineyards *
5. Beringer Vineyards *
6. Cakebread Cellars *
7. Charles Krug Winery *
8. Chateau Montelena *
9. Chimney Rock Winery *
10. Clos du Val *
11. Clos Pegase *
12. Cuvaison Winery *
13. Domaine Carneros *
14. Domaine Chandon *
15. Duckhorn Vineyards
16. Flora Springs Winery
17. Franciscan Oakville Estate
18. Freemark Abbey Winery *
19. Frog's Leap Winery
20. Grgich Hills Cellars *
21. The Hess Collection Winery *
22. Joseph Phelps Vineyards *
23. La Famiglia di Robert Mondavi
24. Livingston Wines
25. Louis M. Martini Winery *
26. Markham Vineyards
27. Merryvale Vineyards
28. Monticello Cellars
29. Mumm Napa Valley *
30. Nichelini Winery
31. Niebaum-Coppola Estate Winery *
32. Pine Ridge Winery
33. Prager Winery & Portworks
34. Robert Mondavi Winery *
35. Robert Sinskey Vineyards

36. Rutherford Hill Winery *
37. St. Clement Vineyards *
38. St. Supéry Vineyards & Winery *
39. Saintsbury
40. Schramsberg Vineyards *
41. Sequoia Grove Vineyard
42. Silverado Vineyards
43. Spottswoode Winery
44. Stag's Leap Wine Cellars *
45. Sterling Vineyards *
46. Sutter Home Winery *
47. Trefethen Vineyards *
48. Turnbull Wine Cellars
49. V. Sattui Winery *
50. ZD Wines

The Operations of a Vineyard Year

January: Weeding, spraying, pruning, vine tying/vine training, major machinery maintenance

February: Pruning, vine tying/vine training, major machinery maintenance, rootstock pulled from nursery/stored, budwood selection/storage

March: Vine tying/vine training, cultivating, discing, frost control

April: Planting rootstock and benchgrafts, cultivating/discing, foliar spraying-fertilization, irrigation, frost

control, suckering (removing undesirable shoots), sulfuring (to prevent mildew), fertilizing, vine tying/vine training

May: Irrigation, foliar spraying on leaves, planting, suckering, cultivating/discing, frost control, fertilizing, vine tying/vine training, sulfuring

June: Foliar spraying on leaves, cultivating/discing, suckering, grafting, irrigation, frost control, crop thinning, fertilizing, vine tying/vine training, sulfuring

July: Cultivating/discing, irrigation vine tying/vine training, berry (actual description of and industry name for grape) sampling

August: Irrigation, hedging, harvesting, grafting, berry sampling, ongoing installation of irrigation and frost control systems, vineyard development operations, soil preparation

September: Harvesting, grafting, berry sampling, ongoing installation of irrigation and frost control systems, vineyard development operations, soil preparation

October: Harvesting, ongoing installation of irrigation and frost control systems, vineyard development operations, soil preparation

November: Major machinery maintenance, weed spraying, chiseling (breaking up soil compaction), ongoing installation of irrigation and frost control systems, vineyard development operations, soil preparation

December: Major machinery maintenance, weed spraying, ongoing installation of irrigation and frost control systems, vineyard development operations, soil preparation

Winery Tours

Wineries by Napa Valley Region

Down-Valley (South)
Artesa Winery

Chimney Rock Winery

Clos du Val

Domaine Carneros

Domaine Chandon

The Hess Collection Winery

Stag's Leap Wine Cellars

Trefethen Vineyards

Mid-Valley (Central)
Beaulieu Vineyards

Cakebread Cellars

Grgich Hills Cellars

Robert Mondavi Winery

Mumm Napa Valley

Niebaum-Coppola Estate
   Winery

Rutherford Hill Winery

St. Supéry Vineyards & Winery

Up-Valley (North)
Beringer Vineyards

Chateau Montelena

Clos Pegase

Cuvaison Winery

Freemark Abbey Winery

Charles Krug Winery

Louis M. Martini Winery

Joseph Phelps Vineyards

St. Clement Vineyards

Schramsberg Vineyards

Sterling Vineyards

Sutter Home Winery

V. Sattui Winery

Wineries by Town

Calistoga
Chateau Montelena

Clos Pegase

Cuvaison Winery

Schramsberg Vineyards

Sterling Vineyards

Napa
Artesa Winery

Chimney Rock Winery

Clos du Val

Domaine Carneros

The Hess Collection Winery

Stag's Leap Wine Cellars

Trefethen Vineyards

Oakville
Robert Mondavi Winery

Rutherford
Beaulieu Vineyards

Cakebread Cellars

Grgich Hills Cellars

Mumm Napa Valley

Niebaum-Coppola Estate
   Winery

Rutherford Hill Winery

St. Supéry Vineyards & Winery

St. Helena
Beringer Vineyards

Freemark Abbey Winery

Charles Krug Winery

Louis M. Martini Winery

Joseph Phelps Vineyards

St. Clement Vineyards

Sutter Home Winery

V. Sattui Winery

Yountville
Domaine Chandon

Ideal Visiting Seasons for Wineries

Winter
Chimney Rock Winery

Domaine Carneros

Freemark Abbey Winery

The Hess Collection Winery

Spring
Artesa Winery

Beringer Vineyards

Domaine Chandon

Charles Krug Winery

Niebaum-Coppola Estate
   Winery

Joseph Phelps Vineyards

Sterling Vineyards

Summer
Chateau Montelena

Clos Pegase

Cuvaison Winery

Grgich Hills Cellars

Louis M. Martini Winery

Rutherford Hill Winery

Schramsberg Vineyards

Stag's Leap Wine Cellars

Sutter Home Winery

V. Sattui Winery

Autumn
Beaulieu Vineyards

Cakebread Cellars

Clos du Val

Robert Mondavi Winery

Mumm Napa Valley

St. Clement Vineyards

St. Supéry Vineyards & Winery

Trefethen Vineyards

Wineries Recommended for Your Special Interests

Attention to Wine with Food
Beringer Vineyards

Cakebread Cellars

Domaine Carneros

Domaine Chandon

Grgich Hills Cellars

Robert Mondavi Winery

Mumm Napa Valley

Niebaum-Coppola Estate
   Winery

Rutherford Hill Winery

St. Supéry Vineyards & Winery

Stag's Leap Wine Cellars

Sterling Vineyards

V. Sattui Winery

CAVES

Beringer Vineyards

Clos Pegase

Rutherford Hill Winery

St. Clement Vineyards

Schramsberg Vineyards

CHAMPAGNE/
SPARKLING WINE

Artesa Winery

Beaulieu Vineyards

Domaine Carneros

Domaine Chandon

Robert Mondavi Winery

Mumm Napa Valley

Schramsberg Vineyards

CONTEMPORARY
ART COLLECTIONS

Artesa Winery

Clos Pegase

The Hess Collection Winery

Robert Mondavi Winery

St. Supéry Vineyards & Winery

CONTEMPORARY OR
SPECIAL ARCHITECTURE

Artesa Winery

Cakebread Cellars

Chimney Rock Winery

Clos Pegase

The Hess Collection Winery

Robert Mondavi Winery

Joseph Phelps Winery

Rutherford Hill Winery

Sterling Vineyards

FRENCH CHATEAU-STYLE
ARCHITECTURE

Chateau Montelena

Domaine Carneros

GARDENS

Beringer Vineyards

Cakebread Cellars

Chateau Montelena

Chimney Rock Winery

Domaine Chandon

Freemark Abbey Winery

Louis M. Martini Winery

Robert Mondavi Winery

Niebaum-Coppola Estate
    Winery

Joseph Phelps Vineyards

St. Clement Vineyards

Schramsberg Vineyards

Stag's Leap Wine Cellars

Sutter Home Winery

Trefethen Vineyards

V. Sattui Winery

OUTSTANDING PANORAMAS

Artesa Winery

Chateau Montelena

Chimney Rock Winery

Domaine Carneros

Charles Krug Winery

Niebaum-Coppola Estate
    Winery

Joseph Phelps Vineyards

Rutherford Hill Winery

Sterling Vineyards

OUTSTANDING TOURS

Domaine Chandon

Robert Mondavi Winery

Mumm Napa Valley

St. Supéry Vineyards & Winery

PICNIC SETTINGS

Beaulieu Vineyards

Clos Pegase

Cuvaison Winery

Freemark Abbey Winery

Louis M. Martini Winery

Joseph Phelps Vineyards

Rutherford Hill Winery

Stag's Leap Wine Cellars

V. Sattui Winery

SELF-TOURS

The Hess Collection Winery

St. Supéry Vineyards & Winery

Sterling Vineyards

Sutter Home Winery

V. Sattui Winery

STAINED GLASS WINDOWS

Beringer Vineyards

St. Clement Vineyards

Sterling Vineyards

VICTORIAN HOMES, INTERIORS

Beringer Vineyards

St. Clement Vineyards

St. Supéry Vineyards & Winery

Sutter Home Winery

VINEYARD TOURS

Cakebread Cellars

Chimney Rock Winery

Clos du Val

Grgich Hills Cellars

Charles Krug Winery

Robert Mondavi Winery

St. Supéry Vineyards & Winery

Trefethen Vineyards

WINE-MAKING EMPHASIS

Cakebread Cellars

Clos du Val

Cuvaison Winery

Domaine Carneros

Domaine Chandon

Grgich Hills Cellars

Charles Krug Winery

Louis M. Martini Winery

Robert Mondavi Winery

Mumm Napa Valley

St. Supéry Vineyards & Winery

Schramsberg Vineyards

Stag's Leap Wine Cellars

Trefethen Vineyards

TRIANGLE TOURS

Three winery tours per day—or fewer—is an ideal scheduling goal for an enjoyable stay in the Napa Valley. This takes into consideration a first tour starting around 10 A.M. and time for lunch at one of the many fine restaurants here or out of your own picnic hamper. Plan time to visit the towns, as well, which offer museums, shopping, and historical attractions that should not be overlooked. Wineries close by 5:30 P.M. at the latest, allowing time to rest before the evening meal.

Below you'll find examples of day-trip winery destinations in geographically balanced "triangles." They're starting points for your imagination. These triangle tours do not take into account specific interests, such as a fascination with Victorian architecture, or a passion for contemporary art, or a yearning to visit gardens. (See recommendations according to these and other interests on p. 24.) Nor do they list specific restaurants in the various regions. For restaurant listings, check with the various Chambers of Commerce or turn to locals for friendly suggestions. I've suggested picnicking when one or more wineries in the suggested triangle offers a comfortable picnic setting.

Remember that the valley's thirty-mile length means at least one hour of driving for a round-trip from either end, from Napa or Calistoga. This shortens the time for touring. You might consider mid-valley accommodations or lodging at one end of the valley one night and the opposite the next. Or zigzag through the valley, cutting through the vineyards on one of the lateral roads off Highway 29 or the Silverado Trail. Bear in mind that, even at its broadest point, the valley is only five miles wide.

Whatever your plans, relax and enjoy every minute of your stay.

FROM DOWN-VALLEY (SOUTH)

- The Hess Collection Winery/lunch in Napa/Trefethen Vineyards/Domaine Chandon
- Clos du Val/Chimney Rock Winery/picnic at Stag's Leap Wine Cellars/Stag's Leap Wine Cellars
- Artesa Winery/Domaine Carneros/late lunch in Napa or Carneros region/The Hess Collection Winery

FROM MID-VALLEY (CENTRAL)

- Robert Mondavi Winery/lunch in Oakville/Cakebread Cellars/Niebaum-Coppola Estate Winery
- St. Supéry Vineyards & Winery/picnic at Rutherford Hill Winery/Rutherford Hill Winery/Mumm Napa Valley
- Niebaum-Coppola Estate Winery/lunch in Oakville or Rutherford or picnic at Beaulieu Vineyards/Beaulieu Vineyards/Grgich Hills Cellars

FROM UP-VALLEY (NORTH)

- Freemark Abbey Winery/lunch in St. Helena/Charles Krug Winery/Beringer Vineyards
- Cuvaison Winery/picnic at Cuvaison Winery or Clos Pegase/Clos Pegase/Sterling Vineyards
- Mumm Napa Valley/Joseph Phelps Vineyards/picnic at Joseph Phelps or at Louis M. Martini Winery/Louis M. Martini Winery
- St. Clement Vineyards/lunch in St. Helena or Calistoga/Schramsberg Vineyards/Sterling Vineyards
- Cakebread Cellars/picnic at V. Sattui Winery/V. Sattui Winery/Sutter Home Winery
- Chateau Montelena/Cuvaison Winery/lunch in Calistoga or picnic at Cuvaison or Clos Pegase/Clos Pegase

ARTESA WINERY

Artesa Winery
1345 Henry Road
Napa, CA 94558
(707) 224-9601
fax (707) 224-5543
Website: www.artesawinery.com
Email: See website

Winemaker: Don Van Staaveren
Winery owner: Codorniu, S.A.

Access

Location: From Highway 29, turn west onto Highway 121 toward Sonoma. After 4 miles, turn right on Old Sonoma Road. After 1 block, turn left on Dealy Lane. Proceed northwest on Dealy Lane, which becomes Henry Road, where the road curves beyond Carneros Creek winery. Turn left into the driveway.

Hours open for visits and tastings: 10 A.M.–5 P.M. daily, except holidays, closed Christmas Eve through New Year's Day. Tours given at 11 A.M. and 2 P.M., other times by appointment.

Appointment necessary for tour? No. Groups by appointment only.

Wheelchairs accommodated? Yes.

Tastings

Charge for tasting with tour? $2 to $8, for tasting of one to five wines, not deductible from price of wine.

Charge for tasting without tour? As above.

Typical wines offered: One sparkling wine, one Chardonnay, one Pinot Noir, and two other seasonal wines.

Sales of wine-related items? Yes.

Picnics and Programs

Picnic area open to the public? No.

Special events or wine-related programs? Carneros Concierge, a service to help guests discover other Carneros wineries.

The sleek, modern elements of Artesa Winery are hidden in the heart of a grassy hill. This, one of Napa Valley's most contemporary wineries in architectural style, was designed to reproduce the form of a previously existing knoll in the Carneros vineyard region. Besides inflicting minimal impact on the countryside, the winery's design harmonizes—in fact meshes—with the surrounding landscape.

The Codorniu family of Barcelona owns this recently renamed winery, formerly known as Codorniu Napa. The family has produced wine since 1551 and was the first family in Spain to create méthode champenoise sparkling wine, in 1872. With such an ancient history, some might expect Moorish arches and Old World architecture for this, the first sparkling and still wine wine-making venture outside Spain for the Codorniu descendants. But, after an original five-year scouting of the grape-growing regions of the world, the decision was to buy land in Carneros and to build a sweepingly modern winery. The enterprise has drawn acclaim since its opening in 1991.

To reach the imposing property, you turn off Old Sonoma Road, very near Domaine Carneros. In fact, one suggestion is to visit both wineries back-to-back so that you can experience the variations in style—architectural as well as enological—between the French and Spanish companies.

On approaching the site, you may have difficulty identifying the estate until you reach the winery signs at the gates. Then comes the great "Aha!"

Yes, the winery is in view all along, but it blends so well with the surroundings that it appears to be one of the many other craggy hills in the area. Due as well to the native California matte fescue grasses planted on the earthen berm covering the facility, the winery hides its face. Once you are on the curving drive to the parking area at the base of the winery, the minimalist architecture by Spaniard Domingo Triay and Napa Valley architect E. R. Bouligny becomes a dominant force, which is sure to hold your attention throughout your stay.

A cascading waterfall cuts the center of the forty-five broad steps you will climb to reach Artesa's entry. The view seems to offer a new and better panorama at each landing during the ascent, culminating in the breathtaking vista from the top of the knoll. There you can see the San Francisco Bay in the distance. Nearer is San Pablo Bay, which hugs the edges of Carneros, bringing with it the famous fog of the region. The same view encompasses Millikin Peak and rolling hills and vineyards, including Artesa's 170 acres of vines (150 acres lie on northern Alexander Valley property).

From the fountains playing at the winery's promontory, you will walk into the sophisticated silence of the winery. A rotating display of resident artist Gordon Huether's striking work decorates walls and corridors, and there is a "Carneros Concierge" center on the side of the tasting room. The concierge service will create a printout of other Carneros region wineries, based on a questionnaire offered to visitors. Since Carneros is such a rapidly growing region, this is a useful service. There, surrounded by elegant wood and metal interiors also designed by Triay, you will be warmly greeted and led on a comprehensive tour. The guide will cover wine making and history including discussion of an ancient barrel and other wine-making artifacts brought from Barcelona. You will walk outside to the two tank presses and then, inside, you will view several thousand French oak barrels as well as the sparkling-wine production line where 175,000 cases are bottled annually. Tours tend to be small in size; between six and ten visitors stroll with the guide. Even if you have entered via the handicapped access, expect some stairs on the tour. You will not actually descend four stories into the ground, but from an upper walkway you will see the aging sparkling wine on pallets. (For a complete discussion of the process of making sparkling wine, please see the chapter on Schramsberg Vineyards.)

There is something at this winery for everyone. You can choose to learn about the technical side of the winery or you may sit on the veranda, sip sparkling brut, Sauvignon Blanc, Chardonnay, or Pinot Noir, and bask in the view.

The Spanish have a saying for it: *"Qué vida tan allegre!"*— what a happy life!

Beaulieu Vineyards

1960 St. Helena Highway
Rutherford, CA 94573
(707) 967-5200
fax (707) 963-5920
Website: www.bvwine.com
Email: See website

Winemaker: Joel Aiken

Winery owner: United Distillers & Vintners (UDV)

Access

Location: On the corner of Rutherford Road (Highway 128) and Highway 29.

Hours open for visits and tastings: Weekdays 10 A.M.–4 P.M., weekends 10 A.M.–5 P.M., closed New Year's Day, Easter, Thanksgiving, and Christmas.

Appointment necessary for tour? No.

Wheelchairs accommodated? Yes.

Tastings

Charge for tasting with tour? Yes.

Charge for tasting without tour? Yes.

Typical wines offered: Sauvignon Blanc, Chardonnay, Cabernet Sauvignon, Pinot Noir, Muscat.

Sales of wine-related items? Yes, including logo glasses ($3 and $4.95).

Picnics and Programs

Picnic area open to the public? No.

Special events or wine-related programs? Beaulieu Wine Society—members receive one to three bottles of wine each month plus discounts at winery and by mail, as well as VIP tour and tasting at winery, with advance reservation, and various special events.

You can learn a tremendous amount about wine making at Beaulieu Vineyards even before the tour begins. On entering the barrel-shaped upper level of the visitors' center of this venerable winery, do be sure to walk the entire perimeter of the area. There are displays of wine-related implements, such as a collection of corkscrews, varying in style from modest to frivolous and dating back to 1900. Other entry-room presentations include one on coopering techniques, most procedures for which have not changed over centuries of barrel making. There is also an excellent corkwood exhibit that demonstrates a cork's passage from tree bark to newly cut, unfinished cork to the finished product: cleaned, champhered (edged), branded, and paraffined.

The tour guide leads you across the shaded parking area to the crush pad behind the winery, which was greatly enlarged in 1969 when members of the original Georges de Latour family sold Beaulieu to Heublein, Inc. During crush, you're at winemaker level watching grapes rain into the steel crush pads, which resemble huge metal V-shaped troughs. Perhaps because of the friendliness between the guides and the winery workers, there is very little sense of a huge corporation here. Although there are relatively few cellarworkers year-round, 400 to 450 pickers are needed at harvest time and production yields nearly a million cases per year.

Next on the tour agenda, the group, which can vary in size from five to about twenty-five, is led to the "Valley of the Redwoods"—the area of the winery where traditional eighty-five-year-old redwood tanks create an aromatic wooden alley. Be sure to note the glass tubing running along the cement walls. With this system, fermented grape juice is pumped in a visible manner from one part of the winery to another, banding the cement stone walls with deep red or pale green, depending on the juices. You'll hear the bottling line activity in the background.

André Tchelistcheff, the revered active winemaker for the winery from 1938 until 1973, stamped his legendary mark on Beaulieu wines. It was he who created the distinguishing hallmark of BV wines by putting the juice of the vineyard into American, rather than French, oak barrels.

The actual winery faces Highway 29, with a wall of ivy and Virginia creeper covering the original brick and concrete building. It dates from 1885 and was owned by Seneca Ewer, one of the prominent landowners who joined the first circle of Napa Valley winemakers. Ewer's sale of the winery to Frenchman Georges de Latour was a fortuitous move for the history of wine making in the Napa Valley, as Latour was an extremely zealous entrepreneur who extended word of his winery (named *beau lieu*, French for "beautiful place") through San Francisco social circles, making the wine a turn-of-the-century favorite.

The tour ends back at the visitors' center with a generous tasting of Beaulieu wines and the option of tasting older wines in the Private Reserve Room. There, one-ounce pours of such vintages as '86, '90, '91, and '95 are sold at a nominal fee of $2.75—a bargain, considering that these wines would normally sell for $70 to $150 per bottle.

BERINGER VINEYARDS

Beringer Vineyards

2000 Main Street
St. Helena, CA 94574
(707) 963-7115
fax (707) 963-1735
Website: www.beringer.com
Email: See website

Winemaker: Ed Sbragia
Winery owner: Beringer Wine Estates

Access

Location: In the northern outskirts of St. Helena on Highway 29 at the "tunnel of elms."

Hours open for visits and tastings: 9:30 A.M.–5 P.M. May 1–October 30; 9:30 A.M.–4 P.M. November 1–April 30, except New Year's Day, Easter, Thanksgiving, and Christmas.

Appointment necessary for tour? No.

Wheelchairs accommodated? Yes.

Tastings

Charge for tasting with tour? No.

Charge for tasting without tour? No. However, there is a $3–$7 fee per glass for reserve wines poured in the Private Reserve Room, not deductible from the price of purchased wine.

Typical wines offered: Complimentary tasting of Napa Valley Chardonnay, White Zinfandel, and Cabernet Sauvignon. Private Reserve Room tastings may include Napa Valley Reserve Chardonnay, Viognier, Cabernet Sauvignon, Knight's Valley Alluvium, and Howell Mountain Merlot.

Sales of wine-related items? Yes, including logo glasses ($9.50).

Picnics and Programs
Picnic area open to the public? No.

Special events or wine-related programs? Wine release festivals in spring and fall.

At Beringer, you can visit an elegant Victorian home, photograph seasonal flower beds, or explore century-old tunnels for wine aging. This winery has generated vintages since 1876, earning it the title of Napa Valley's oldest winery with continuous production. Even during Prohibition, the Beringer family was granted approval to produce sacramental and medicinal wines and brandies when other companies closed their doors. Because of its lengthy history and recognition, hundreds of thousands of tourists have journeyed to the valley with Beringer as their specific goal.

On turning onto the estate grounds, you will first see the impressive seventeen-room Rhine House, built in the 1880s. The Beringer brothers—businessman Frederick and winemaker Jacob—built the home to resemble their birthplace in Mainz, Germany. The slate roof, European stained glass windows, and intricately inlaid wooden floors are all original, as is most of the home, which was restored after 1971 when the winery was purchased by Nestlé, Inc. Then, under ownership of the Texas Pacific Group, the winery became a publicly traded company in 1997.

The walk south from the parking lot will lead you past the Hudson House, Jacob's home, where he, his wife, and their six children lived. It now houses Beringer's private Culinary Arts Center. Visitors usually find the the spring-flowering wisteria, azaleas, oleanders, and roses on the Beringer grounds unforgettable. If photography is your hobby, be sure to have film for this visit. Visitors who don't choose to follow the tour may enjoy a complimentary tasting of three wines in the Old Bottling Room.

Due to the popularity of this winery tour, delays are frequent. However, tours begin every half-hour in the tour center on the terrace. Below is Ruth Asawa's delightful bronze fountain that depicts the history of wine making.

Inside the center, you will sit on benches, joining thirty to forty other tourists. The tour guide will review the history of the Beringer family and the winery, pointing to such historical photos as one of Hollywood stars Charles Laughton and Carole Lombard celebrating the end of Prohibition in 1933 at Beringer.

While strolling up the gentle slope backing the center, you'll learn of the hundred Chinese laborers who were hired to chisel a thousand feet of tunnels from the Spring Mountain foothills just west of the Hudson House. On that site, Jacob oversaw the construction of a gravity-flow winery, 104 feet long by 40 feet wide. It was completed in 1876. Although Beringer now makes wine in a more modern facility directly across Highway 29, the renowned Cabernet Sauvignons are aged in French oak barrels within Jacob's original tunnels. Don't miss the hand-carved German barrels near the tunnel entrances.

The tour meanders through the tunnels, which have been restructured for seismic purposes but still impart a sense of the original cellars. There is even a wine library, which houses vintages as old as 1937, dusty with time.

No vineyard is visited on the tour; however, you will see demonstration vines showing the growth of Chardonnay, Cabernet, Sauvignon Blanc, and Merlot grapes, all of which are important for production of the winery's varietal wines.

Down in the main gardens, the "Soaked Oak" holds forth in a prominent corner. Branches of the massive deciduous oak tree curl back on each other like a corkscrew. Some tour guides say that roots of the two-hundred-plus-year-old tree stretched under the caves and up into barrels of wine to cause the tree's contorted form.

The last stop on the Beringer tour is the former dining room in the Rhine House. There you will taste three wines—perhaps four if port is poured. Take time to study the stained glass windows in that room and throughout the house; Beringer holds the finest stained glass collection in the Napa Valley. Insurance coverage on the Rhine House alone is now more than $6 million, a far cry from the original $28,000 construction costs for the entire Germanic Victorian. The main rooms of the home are open for inspection, including an upper bedroom now dubbed the Founders' Room, where special reserve wines are poured.

Guides at Beringer are the only ones in the valley to toast visitors as they taste wine. "To your health!" or "Have a great time in the valley!" are frequent salutes, accompanied by clinking glasses. Guests are encouraged to drink wine at home, even with simple family fare. By the time you walk back to the parking area, you'll have a deeper understanding of Victorian times and how wine making related to life then as well as now.

Cakebread Cellars

8300 St. Helena Highway
Rutherford, CA 94573
(707) 963-5221
fax (707) 963-1067
Website: www.cakebread.com
Email: cellars@cakebread.com

Winemaker: Bruce Cakebread
Winery owners: Jack and Dolores Cakebread

Access

Location: On the east side of Highway 29, slightly over ½ mile north of Robert Mondavi Winery; look for stone walls and colorful flower beds.

Hours open for visits and tastings: 10 A.M.–4 P.M. daily, except New Year's Day, Easter, Thanksgiving, and Christmas.

Appointment necessary for tour? Yes; call 24 hours in advance or early the same morning.

Wheelchairs accommodated? Yes.

Tastings

Charge for tasting with tour? No.

Charge for tasting without tour? Yes; two tasting programs.

Typical wines offered: Current vintages of Sauvignon Blanc, Chardonnay, Merlot, Pinot Noir, Rubaiyat (proprietary blend), Cabernet Sauvignon.

Two reserve wines: Benchland Select and Three Sisters Cabernet Sauvignon.

Sales of wine-related items? Logo glasses and clothing.

Picnics and Programs

Picnic area open to the public? No.

Special events or wine-related programs? No.

Among the myriad wineries along the road between Napa and Calistoga, Cakebread Cellars stands out in a colorful way. In any season of the year, look for masses of flowers in bloom on the east side of the road in Rutherford, just about halfway along the thirty-mile stretch.

The exuberance of the flowers is mirrored in the strong family spirit that greets all visitors. A joyful work ethic has been passed from winery founders Jack and Dolores Cakebread to their children and on to the winery staff, and through them to winery visitors.

The winery tour starts in the vineyard. There the informative, low-key tour opens with talk of the importance of the right land to grow the best grapes. "At an average cost of one hundred thousand dollars an acre or more, Napa Valley floor land is the second most expensive farm soil in the United States," notes the tour guide, who is swift to mention that the most expensive farmland is in Riverside, California. He notes that grapes are second only to cotton in agricultural importance to the state of California, where 75 percent of the nation's wine grapes, 90 percent of its table grapes, and 100 percent of its raisin grapes are grown. "But all the vineyards combined in the Napa Valley only grow 6 percent of those wine grapes, and the first cash crop of grapes doesn't mature until four to five years after the rootstock is planted," he says, putting a realistic note on the thousands of rows of vines stretching the width of the valley.

There are now more than 250 use permits and 172 bonded, licensed wineries in the Napa Valley, but when Jack Cakebread decided to plant grapes in 1972, his was winery license number 38. At the time, he and his wife bought land just north of Oakville from elderly friends named Sturdivant with the understanding that the friends could live out their days on the property. Then when the Cakebreads came on board, they created a true mom-and-pop operation, with mechanical know-how and a strong sense of design from Jack and culinary savvy with a nutritious slant from Dolores. They frequently travel to promote their Cabernet Sauvignon, Sauvignon Blanc, and Chardonnay.

Although the winery has grown from its early stages to a seventy-two-acre property with production of fifty thousand cases a year, it retains the hands-on feeling and remains a family project. Son Bruce is now the Cakebread winemaker; Dennis works as business manager for the company; and third son Steven, an executive for an electronics firm in Singapore, is a member of the board of directors for the winery. Dolores has developed a culinary program for visiting chefs and wine writers to encourage them to be aware of local produce and other Napa Valley food resources and how to pair them with wine. Also, she oversees the floral welcome at the winery's entrance.

"This is a working winery. Please stay together as we tour the production area," admonishes the tour guide as you join a group of ten visitors in the air-conditioned building. The winery buildings, designed by William Turnbull, present a contemporary redwood barn architecture that blends easily into the landscape. Engineering buffs are intrigued with the ultra-modern equipment, which offers such practical systems as a drainage process that allows a simultaneous hosing of machines, vats, walls, and floors as well as an air flow program that reduces electrical costs.

In the storage room, instructions for how to read notations, the brand marks and pencil jottings on a wine barrel, are clearly explained. "Here," says the tour guide pointing to one end of a barrel, "is the barrel maker's name. This notes the source of the wood. Next, the year the barrel was bought, followed by the wine initials [C.S. for Cabernet Sauvignon, for example] and finally the vintage and any special comments, such as ML for malolactic fermentation."

The guide fields all questions, such as how the winemaker balances the oak influences in flavoring the fermented grape juice. "Believe me," he says, "the last thing we want is wine with the flavor of Chateau Two-by-Four! Too much wood can be a real negative for wines which are made to lay down a long while."

There is no pressure to return to the tasting room, though most do so readily. Most tourists have gone out of their way to visit Cakebread for specific reasons, such as to tour the source of a bottle of wine opened to celebrate their anniversary or at their favorite restaurant. One tourist said, "It's nice to find out that the Cakebreads are real people who like their wine and their work . . . and beautiful flowers."

CHATEAU MONTELENA

Chateau Montelena

1429 Tubbs Lane
Calistoga, CA 94515
(707) 942-5105
fax (707) 942-4221
Website: www.montelena.com
Email: See website

Winemaker: James P. "Bo" Barrett
Winery owner: James L. Barrett,
Managing General Partner

Access

Location: 2 miles north of Lincoln
Avenue in Calistoga (at the flashing
red light at Lincoln Avenue), turn
right (if driving north) onto Tubbs
Lane.

Hours open for visits and tastings:
10 A.M.–4 P.M. daily, except Good
Friday, Easter, Saturday of
Memorial Day weekend, Memorial
Day, Fourth of July, Labor Day,
Christmas through New Year's.

Appointment necessary for tour? Yes.
Tours at 11 A.M. and 2 P.M.

Wheelchairs accommodated? Yes,
except in unpaved parking lot.

Tastings

Charge for tasting with tour? $5 for
three wines, price discounted from
purchase of over $20.

Charge for tasting without tour?
As above.

Typical wines offered: Chardonnay,
Cabernet Sauvignon, and
Johannisberg Riesling; when
available, Zinfandel.

Sales of wine-related items? Yes.

Picnics and Programs

Picnic area open to the public? No.

Special events or wine-related
programs? Annual Open House first
weekend in March.

Special customers receive notification of
wines before release and are invited
to a private party in the spring.

In the manner of the faithful geyser up the road from Chateau Montelena, a discrete, major spurt in the wine world brought this Napa Valley winery to prominence. That burst of energy came in June 1976, when for the first time, the wines of California overcame the grapes of Gaul. During a critical blind tasting judged in Paris by nine French oenophiles, California wines topped those of France, with Chateau Montelena '73 as the champion Chardonnay.

The judges could not have been more amazed. What might have surprised them as well is that this winery is housed in a building of truly Gallic origins. Designed after the great chateaux of Bordeaux and built by a French architect, this was one of the small, thriving wineries of the early 1900s. Winery walls are three to twelve feet thick, made of imported and native cut stone. Senator Alfred Tubbs, originally a Bostonian, was the owner who chose the French design of what was then the sixth largest winery in the valley.

The rustic redwood tasting room that you'll see on arrival gives little hint of the splendid chateau beneath it. The visitors' room is located on an upper floor in the rear of the chateau, but appreciation of the tradition and architecture of this winery demands making the short walk downhill, to

properly view the ivy-covered stone facade of this elegant estate. There is a splendid vista point from man-made Jade Lake, which fronts the chateau. From there, you'll view the chateau, the willow-framed lake, and the quaint red lacquered bridge that spans the lake from the shore to the pavilions on an island.

Beyond the lake lie acres of Chateau Montelena vineyards, the home of Jim Barrett—who dubs himself a "caretaker of the land" instead of its owner—and Mount St. Helena, rising two thousand feet in the background. Some say this is the Napa Valley dream view; it is definitely a photo opportunity to consider seriously. Wildlife aficionados will find ducks, swans, turtles, catfish, and a number of wild birds using the island as a sanctuary. Considering the heady floral perfume that laces summer's hot, dry air, thoughts of Monet's garden at Giverny may jump to mind. Cascading old-fashioned roses vie with flora and fauna in the full spectrum of colors and bouquets. In fact, there is a similar, idyllic quality to time spent chez Monet and at this winery.

Along one of the lakeside paths there is a plaque proclaiming an ancient Chinese proverb: "Peace and tranquility to all who enter here." The aphorism was placed by former owners Yort and Jeanne Frank, who lived in the chateau after Prohibition forced closure of the business. Now the chateau is used for winery purposes only. Present owner Barrett, whose son Bo is winemaker, offers the same four varietals today as in 1972: Cabernet Sauvignon, Zinfandel, Chardonnnay, and Riesling. Barrett says his background as an attorney gave him the proper perspective on a life in the wine industry: "I spent eighteen years giving pain to people," he explains. "Now I spend my life giving them pleasure."

Pleasure they do receive. During a post-tour tasting, a visitor from Miami explained that she particularly enjoys the winery's Riesling, which is sold only in-house, because "it's not high in tannin that would make me want a drink after I've had a drink."

And what of the famous Chateau Montelena Chardonnay, made with grapes grown in volcanic and sedimentary soils in the Oak Knoll district of Napa Valley? It is still one of the most popular wines tasted and purchased at the winery, even years after the touted Paris tasting, and second only to the Montelena Estate Cabernet Sauvignon.

Wine is not all that visitors take with them on departing the chateau. One tour guide notes, "Most people come like pilgrims to taste the Chardonnay or Cabernet, and when they get here, the beauty of the place adds to the whole experience and they leave refreshed."

Chimney Rock Winery

5350 Silverado Trail
Napa, CA 94558
(707) 257-2641
fax (707) 257-2036
Website: www.chimneyrock.com
Email: retail@chimneyrock.com

Winemaker: Douglas Fletcher
Winery owners: Sheldon and Stella
Wilson

Access

Location: 5 miles north of Napa on
the Silverado Trail, just north of the
Chimney Rock Golf Course.

Hours open for visits and tastings:
10 A.M.–4 P.M. daily, except
Easter, Thanksgiving, and
Christmas.

Appointment necessary? Yes.

Wheelchairs accommodated?
Yes, except on tour.

Tastings

Charge for tasting with tour? $5.

Charge for tasting without tour? $3.

Typical wines offered: Current and
older vintages of Fumé Blanc and
Cabernet Sauvignon.

Sales of wine-related items?
Yes, including shirts, wine
accessories, and etched bottles for
special occasions.

Picnics and Programs

Picnic area open to the public? No.

Special events or wine-related
programs? No.

The iron gates that open onto Chimney Rock's driveway point the way to one of Napa Valley's more splendid views. Your eye moves from the valley floor up to the eastern hillside, where trellised vineyards stretch along the undulating earth. With or without leaves, the rows of vines follow the various curves and openings in the land. The property seems to stretch forever.

To the right of the entry road, the winery and hospitality center welcome guests for tours. Even though reservations are required, visitors are welcome to join weekday tours of the seventeenth-century-style Cape Dutch buildings. An interesting twist on wine tasting is that you'll be offered a glass of the winery's Chardonnay and Fumé Blanc before tour departure, with the suggestion to "bring along your glass as we walk." This touch enhances the feeling that visitors are sauntering about a gracious home, although Chimney Rock owners Hack and Stella Wilson actually live on the crest of a hill behind the property.

The South African Huguenot style of the Cape Dutch property is unique in the Napa Valley. The graceful roofline curves are particularly visible from the road before early summer, when the poplars that line the estate act as leafless sentinels, giving a full view of the various buildings on the estate.

The tour starts at the hearth in the well-lit entry room. Antique fireplace tools decorate the white walls. Occasionally the tour will include a visit to the private tasting room where an imposing seventeenth-century highboy from South Africa dominates one white wall. That and the other blanched walls of the hospitality center contrast with the rich tones of antique wooden tables, light fixtures, and accent pieces adorning the space. The chalky walls are a refreshing change from the more typical use of unadorned wood in wineries built in the Napa Valley over the last thirty years.

The tour moves outside to a shaded area where sunken waterfalls divide part of the generous patio. From there you'll have a full view of the frieze mounted atop the winery's back wall. The subject of this nine-by-thirty-eight-foot work of art is Ganymede, cup bearer to the gods. The eighteenth-century German sculptor Anton Anreith created the original for the Groot Constantia winery at the Cape Colony of Africa, where Anreith was employed by the Dutch East India Company. To duplicate the masterpiece for Chimney Rock, the Wilsons commissioned California sculptor Michael Casey, resident restoration artist for the state capitol in Sacramento. Imagine mounting the fiberglass-reinforced concrete duplication, which weighs five tons!

Moving to the vineyards and then to the winery, you'll soon realize that this is one of the valley's small wineries. With only nine full-time employees, chances are strong that you'll meet Doug Fletcher, the winemaker, and that you'll be able to speak with him about his wines, which are made strictly in the French manner. Cabernet Sauvignon, Merlot, Cabernet Franc, and Petit Verdot grapes are all used to create Bordeaux-style wines.

If you feel misty while tasting the wine, the cause might be the winery's *faux cave* system of creating constant humidity by spraying a fine fog over the thousand aging barrels, which will yield fifteen thousand cases of wine.

As Cabernet Sauvignon and other vintages are served at

the wine tasting bar, the story is recounted of how friendship with wine expert Alexis Lichine led Hack Wilson—a former hotelier and soft drink and beer marketer—to his 1980 purchase of Chimney Rock Golf Course in the Stags Leap District. Nine holes of the golf course still remain, but the Wilsons had the other nine holes bulldozed (about seventy-five acres). They planted their vineyard estate there based on Lichine's dictate to "look at all of the regions, but when you buy, buy in Napa Valley, for Napa is to California what Bordeaux is to France."

Some would say they scored a hole-in-one by doing so.

CLOS DU VAL

Clos du Val

5330 Silverado Trail
Napa, CA 94558
(707) 259-2225
fax (707) 252-6125
Website: www.closduval.com
Email: cdv@closduval.com

Winemaker: Bernard Portet
Winery owner: John Goelet

Access

Location: 5 miles north of Napa on
the east side of the Silverado Trail.

Hours open for visits and tastings:
10 A.M.–5 P.M. daily, except New
Year's Day, Easter, Thanksgiving,
and Christmas.

Appointment necessary for tour?
Yes; call one to two days in
advance.

Wheelchairs accommodated? Yes.

Tastings

Charge for tasting with tour? No.

Charge for tasting without tour? $5.

Typical wines offered: Cabernet
Sauvignon, Semillon, Chardonnay,
Pinot Noir, Zinfandel, Merlot,
Sangiovese.

Sales of wine-related items?
Yes, including logo glasses ($6.50),
and T-shirts; also, Ronald Searle
winery cartoon posters.

Picnics and Programs
Picnic area open to the public? Yes.

Special events or wine-related
programs? Cellar Club: Pre-release
wine discounted to members before
release to general distributors.
Annual Reserve Debut Event.

The massive doors to the Clos du Val tasting room open to a cool visitors' room, a welcome contrast to the hundred-degree heat of a Napa Valley summer day. This room touts a twenty-eight-foot ceiling and a feeling of space to match the size of the front door. Here you'll find a collection of vintages since 1972 and friendly people proud of their work.

It is from the cavernous tasting room that tours depart, directly to the vineyards. This is a winery seriously involved with the land and in explaining the annual struggle with the soil to produce top-quality grapes. Tours are usually small—two to eight people—and they cover all stages of viticulture and enology.

The view from the vineyards, the tourists' first stop, is exceptional: you are surrounded by acres of vineyards, many edged with roses.

"See those roses?" asked one Clos du Val tour guide, pointing to rosebushes laden with red and yellow blossoms. "There is a Bordeaux tradition that says if the roses bear many blossoms, there will be a strong harvest." This is one explanation for the roses seen frequently bordering vineyards. An alternate explanation is that the buds act like canaries in a coal mine; if the birds weaken, miners take heed and head for a safer area. In this case, if the roses droop or show signs of disease, the grower will inspect the soil or rootstock for disease. Both rose stories have their roots in France, as does Bernard Portet, the winery's first winemaker. Portet is the son of the former *régisseur* of Chateau Lafite, and he instills his love of French oak by insisting on French Nevers and Allier oak barrels for aging wine. The Cabernets are kept in oak for about two years.

The vineyard tour takes you right to the soil that was once a lava bed. If you want to walk between the vines, you will. This is not a dainty sandal tour, unless you don't mind shaking out a few pebbles. If the grapes are at an edible stage, be assured you'll taste some.

Moving from the vineyards, you'll learn of the Clos du Val lands dotting various regions of the Napa Valley: Stags Leap District (where the winery is situated); State Lane, in Yountville; and the Carneros region. Cabernet Sauvignon, Merlot, Zinfandel, Semillon, Cabernet Franc, Pinot Noir, and Chardonnay grapes are bases for the Clos du Val wines as well as Sangiovese under the Tre Grazie label.

If you happen to visit in the early summer, you may be able to view ice on the outside of the stainless steel fermenters, indicating the Chardonnay or "Ariadne" is being cold-stabilized, a process pioneered at Clos du Val.

Just in case all this discussion leaves you out in the cold, a few words from winemaker Portet about how cold stabilization works: "We drop the wine temperature to twenty-eight degrees and leave it there so tartrate crystals will precipitate out here in the winery and not in the bottle at home." You may have seen residue at the bottom of wine bottles—those "flakes" are often tartrates. They're not harmful, but they are not attractive, and this is why many wineries follow the practice of freezing, followed by light filtration.

For an unusual diversion, watch the barrel cleaner in action. When needed, it is fixed on the floor in an alley between layers of barrels. When a high-pressure sprinkler is turned on inside the barrel, the barrel spins as if by magic. This is a reminder of the frivolously entertaining mechanical water gardens outside of Salzburg, but on a practical level.

The tour guide offers an excellent explanation of how to "read" a barrel and, more importantly for the home consumer, how to read a wine label. The latter instruction takes place back at the wine tasting bar in the visitors' center. While there, you may also hear about Taltarni Vineyards in Australia. That is due to the fact that the same owner, John Goelet, owns both properties. Dominique Portet, the brother of Clos du Val's winemaker, Bernard, was the former winemaker in Australia.

While enjoying the various wines, don't miss the collection of droll cartoons lightening the subject of wine. These full-color, framed originals by Ronald Searle hang on a wall near the huge entry door. They were commissioned by John Goelet. I have observed tourists, glass of wine in hand, reading the cartoon wall and laughing out loud, thus enjoying two of life's finest pleasures. Three, if you count visiting the Napa Valley.

Clos Pegase
1060 Dunaweal Lane
Calistoga, CA 94515
(707) 942-4981
fax (707) 942-4993
Website: www.clospegase.com
Email: cp@clospegase.com

Winemaker: Steven Rogstad
Winery owners: Jan and
Mitsuko Shrem

Access
Location: On Highway 29, 7 miles
north of St. Helena, turn northeast
(right, if driving north from St.
Helena) at Dunaweal Lane. The
winery is on the left after .7 miles,
across from the entrance to Sterling
Vineyards.

Hours open for visits and tastings:
10:30 A.M.–5 P.M. daily, except
New Year's Day, Thanksgiving,
Christmas Eve, and Christmas.

Appointment necessary for tour?
Yes, for guided tour of extensive art
collection and caves; not for self-
guided tour.

Wheelchairs accommodated? Yes.

Tastings
Charge for tasting with tour? $2.50.

Charge for tasting without tour?
As above.

Typical wines offered: Chardonnay,
Cabernet, Merlot, and "Hommage"
Reserve Cabernet Sauvignon.

Sales of wine-related items? Yes.

Picnics and Programs
Picnic area open to the public?
Yes, on the lawn; no picnic tables.

Special events or wine-related
programs? The third Saturday of
each month at 2 P.M., a free slide
presentation on 4,000 years of
wine in art by Jan Shrem.

Clos Pegase is a haven for lovers of art and antiquities. A visit to the winery demonstrates the lengths to which owners Jan and Mitsuko Shrem have gone to create a showplace for their Cabernets, Chardonnnays, and other wines.

Before zeroing in on the final design of their winery, the owners initiated a national architectural design competition sponsored by the San Francisco Museum of Modern Art. The winery opened in 1987. Since then, Clos Pegase has garnered numerous international awards for architect and Princeton University professor Michael Graves. His winning design, a Greco-Roman temple to wine and the arts, makes an impressive statement from the moment you drive onto the estate. Contemporary sculpture in the parking lot says it all: art reigns here. In fact, for frequent Clos Pegase visitors the tour guide will point out the latest additions to the collection, such as Jacques Lipschitz' *Bellerophon Taming Pegasus*, Henry Moore's *Mother Earth*, Cesare Peverelli's *The Urban Gent*, or the giant bronze thumb by Cesar that rises out of the vineyards abutting the winery property.

Guests are welcome to sit on the grounds to picnic, according to Jan Shrem. "I want people to feel the connection between wine, food, and the arts," he says with a sweeping gesture of his hand.

Various public rooms at the winery run the gamut from the Harvest Room, thus named due to giant enlargements of vineyard scenes from the medieval *Book of Hours* that adorn the walls, to well-lit caves lined with ancient Bacchanalian statuary. It is in one of the caves that Shrem offers the public a monthly slide show of wine as it has been depicted in art over 4,000 years.

While strolling from the tasting room through the winery caves and back again, tourists can't miss informative boards with key wine-in-art works related to wine in portraiture; wine in mythology; wine and religion; wine as a love potion; wine and the still life; and wine vessels, from the ancient to the contemporary.

Watch for these other outstanding features while on tour:
- the winemaker's laboratory, a little masterpiece of practical contemporary architecture and built-in cabinetry bathed in northeastern light
- the three-hundred-year-old oak tree framed by the two axes of the winery
- terra-cotta tiles covering the winery's floor, lending unity with the Greco-Roman building style; there's even a wine gutter cut into the tiles along the tasting room floor
- the tall barrels beyond the tasting room window wall, reproductions of wine-aging vats found in ancient Roman drawings; they were constructed of French oak in the United States
- the massive single column that dominates the entrance to the winery. Is it supportive or purely an artistic statement?

A number of visitors are curious about the winery's name. Why Pegasus as a "mascot"? Shrem's response is that he and his wife wished to reflect the mythological beginning of wine. According to the legends, Pegasus, the winged horse of Greek mythology, gave birth to wine and the arts when his hooves unleashed the sacred Spring of the Muses. The spring waters tapped roots of the vines and thus inspired the artists and poets who drank the fruit of the vine.

"Clos," in French, connotes any enclosed space. As a Napa Valley winery, Clos Pegase is not just any enclosed space—it is unique.

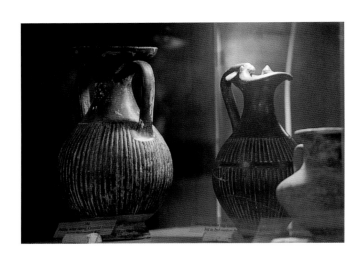

Cuvaison Winery

4550 Silverado Trail
Calistoga, CA 94515
(707) 942-6266
fax (707) 942-5732
Website: www.cuvaison.com
Email: info@cuvaison.com

Winemaker: John Thacher
Winery owner:
Thomas Schmidheiny

Access

Location: From Highway 29, 6 miles north of St. Helena and 2 miles south of Calistoga, take Dunaweal Lane to the Silverado Trail. Turn right; the winery is 500 yards ahead on the left.

Hours open for visits and tastings: 10 A.M.–5 P.M. daily, except New Year's Day, Easter, Thanksgiving, Christmas Eve, and Christmas.

Appointment necessary for winery and cave tour? Yes.

Wheelchairs accommodated? Yes.

Tastings

Charge for tasting with tour? $4 includes logo glass; not deductible from price of purchased wine.

Charge for tasting without tour? As above.

Typical wines offered: Chardonnay, Cabernet Sauvignon, Merlot, Pinot Noir, Zinfandel, and Reserve Chardonnay (all offered as available).

Sales of wine-related items? Yes.

Picnics and Programs

Picnic area open to the public? Yes.

Special events or wine-related programs? Yes.

There is an unassuming quality about Cuvaison Winery. It sits hillside on the Silverado Trail in view of Sterling and around the knoll from Clos Pegase. Three dormant volcanos are within sight—Mount St. Helena, Mount George, and the Mayacamas. Oaks and evergreens border the mission-style winery and a stand of picnic tables awaits warm-weather use. In winter, a wood-burning stove in the visitors' center offers a toasty welcome.

Since it opened in 1970, the winery has evolved at an even pace. As a result, an occasional visit can give the sense of observing a favorite nephew sprouting from an elfin kindergartener to a complex young man. Compared to a visit at a venerable winery, this is like a work in progress. For instance, the cozy tasting room and hospitality center that welcome you on entrance to the winery property used to house the entire winery facility, in the early seventies. Then, Cuvaison was a new tax write-off for the two engineers who owned it. Another sign of evolution includes activity in the building that houses fermentation tanks—it is now jammed to the walls with equipment, and outside, six-by-six-foot Pinot Noir tanks have sprouted like Topsy on the back driveway, as winemaker John Thacher increases his interest in Pinot Noir.

The winery is now quite successful, based on years of radical change and strong management. In 1979, members of the Schmidheiny family of Switzerland, which owns Swatch watches and Tobler chocolates, among other concerns, took ownership and brought a renewed sense of dedication to Cuvaison.

Thacher has replanted hillside vines with Rutherford-area grapes from the Napa Valley floor. The result has been a move from tannic wines best enjoyed in the future to wines drinkable now as well as those able to be laid down.

What is most interesting about touring Cuvaison (which translates from French as "the fermenting of juice on the grape skins in order to extract color") is the sense of seeing evolution in action. In 1992, a new vineyard was planted to offer visitors a chance both to observe various trellising techniques for vine maintenance and to pick and taste grapes during harvest.

Most wineries with memorable tours are relatively large, and their tour styles are quite established. Cuvaison is more informal, beginning with its welcoming approach. The background music in the hospitality room is usually light rock or jazz. The tour guides have been affiliated with the winery for years, and they impart information with a relaxed style, on subjects including winery production and how to read the chalk identification notes scratched on French oak barrels.

As an unusual touch, tourists are given a taste of wine right out of a fermentation vat. Other wineries might offer a barrel tasting, but Cuvaison tour guides open the spigot alongside a vertical tank and pour right into the glass.

"Most of our barrels are housed in two other warehouses in St. Helena and Napa," points out tour guide Janet Behr as the tour passes metal gantries (pallets) holding top-grade French oak barrels. Near the barrel storage area the bottling line rattles along, with views onto the valley through the work station windows.

From watching the bottling action—literally within reach on the tour—you'll move to the wine library, a sophisticated corridor of a room with hundreds of Cuvaison bottles resting in diamond-shaped wooden shelving. The lighting is subtle and the room lends itself to final questions related to the tour. The tour's progression from the simple beginnings of the original winery to the modern surroundings of the wine library seems appropriate for this winery, which continues to reach ever-higher goals.

DOMAINE CARNEROS

The classic elegance of the eighteenth-century chateau that houses Domaine Carneros' sparkling-wine-making facility draws instant attention from travelers in the southwestern tip of the Carneros district of the Napa Valley. Here, in an area frequently blanketed by fog from nearby San Pablo Bay, the modern castle presides on a hill at the vineyard edge. Among American vineyards, it is an international nexus.

Domaine Carneros itself is a partnership of the Taittinger Champagne house of Reims, France, as well as Kobrand Corporation and other partners. The grapes, grown immediately to the north, are used in making Winery Lake and Sterling vintages for Seagram's, the Canadian spirits company. Spain holds forth behind the di Rosa property: almost out of view due to its minimalist architecture, Artesa's profile hints to those who search the hills. Finally, south of Domaine Carneros lie the Swiss vineyards of Cuvaison.

Since the first area infusion of French funds, with the purchase of Domaine Chandon in 1973, the Napa Valley has seen major construction and growth owing to its international support. In most cases, the recently built wineries have demonstrated modern architectural styling. But in the case of Domaine Carneros this is not so.

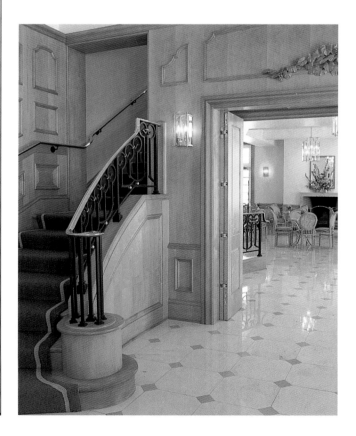

This winery is patterned after the Taittinger-owned Chateau de la Marquetterie in Champagne. Seventy-two steps, broken by occasional landings, lead to the broad stone terrace and entry of the winery. (There is a clearly designated secondary entrance for those intimidated by the stairway.) The first impression once inside is of the grandeur of the place: high ceilings, a graceful staircase, and well-appointed furnishings balance with local limestone and French marble floors.

Follow your eyes into the tasting room at the north wing of the "chateau." It is there that you will join a tour group to see the inner workings of the winery, as well as to learn the background on the French link with Domaine Carneros.

"The fireplace mantel is a Louis XVI piece brought from France, as is this painting of Madame de Pompadour, mistress of Louis XV," says the tour guide. The story goes that a fortune-teller alerted Madame de Pompadour's father that his daughter was to be the mistress of the king. As a result, the gentleman trained his daughter for life in court. That meant he made certain she knew how to read and write in order to mesh easily with the literate lords and ladies of Louis XV's inner circle. This painting, which commands the foyer and which formerly hung at the Hotel Crillon in Paris, depicts Madame de Pompadour with books and sheet music.

From that historical discussion, you will move into a video presentation about the vineyard year for Pinot Noir and Chardonnay, the two grapes ideal for sparkling wine. An excellent segment explains the budding process used on the rootstock. At the video's conclusion, the wide screen is raised and behind a large window you will see a "forest" of stainless steel fermentation tanks, a practical extension of the winemaking procedures covered on film.

From there, a short staircase leads down to a viewing platform from which the guide will point out the continuing stages of *méthode champenoise*, the double-fermentation sparkling-wine process that creates effervescence in the wine. This includes riddling, which primarily is done by mechanical methods despite winemaker Eileen Crane's inclusion of hand-riddling at the winery. You'll also see the disgorging-dosage-corking-cleaning-neck-foiling-labeling bottling line, which is extremely modern equipment in comparison with the antique bottlers on display on the platform.

"Remember," laughs the guide, "the lower the alcohol content, the lower the calories—and sparkling wine has a total of only 12 percent alcohol. I call it a sumptuous diet drink!"

As the group follows along, they learn that ultraviolet light prematurely ages sparkling wine, which is why the aging area—where the wine is aged twenty months—is rather dimly lit. Because the winery was built on top of a knoll, the temperature in the underground aging area simulates cave temperature. This architectural technique frequently is employed to reduce air-conditioning costs as much as to effect cavelike conditions.

In the design of this opulent setting, even the rest rooms received detailed attention. These are the best-appointed rest rooms in the valley.

Back upstairs, Domaine Carneros wine is sold by the glass or by the bottle, accompanied by tasty appetizers. Despite formal surroundings, the tasting room staff is warm and genial.

There is a sense of the civilized life that arises from sitting on French-style chairs, listening to classical music, and sipping Napa Valley sparkling wine, overlooking the hills of Carneros. Whether you visit wearing jeans or summer finery, be prepared to feel like royalty.

Domaine Chandon

Domaine Chandon
1 California Drive
Yountville, CA 94599
(707) 944-2280
fax (707) 944-1123
Restaurant: 800-736-2892
Website: www.chandon.com
Email: dchandon@napanet.net

Winemaker: Dawnine Dwyer
Winery owner:
Moët-Hennessey–Louis Vuitton

Access
Location: Off Highway 29 at
Yountville. From the Veterans Home
exit, go southwest on California
Drive; turn right.

Hours open for visits and tastings:
May through October 10 A.M.–8
P.M. Wednesday to Sunday, 10
A.M.–6 P.M. Monday and Tuesday;
November through April 10 A.M.–
6 P.M. Wednesday to Sunday, closed
Monday and Tuesday. Call for
restaurant hours.

Appointment necessary for tour?
No, except for groups of 16 or more.

Wheelchairs accommodated? Yes.

Tastings
Charge for tasting with tour? $3

Charge for tasting without tour?
As above.

Typical wines offered: Brut,
Blanc de Noir, and Reserve.

Sales of wine-related items? Yes.

Picnics and Programs
Picnic area open to the public?
No (restaurant on property).

Special events or wine-related
programs? Quarterly newsletter,
Chandon Club and Private Cellar
Wine Club, both with special events
and other benefits.

The marriage of past and present in a Napa Valley winery is best demonstrated at Domaine Chandon, on the western side of Yountville, with its sparkling-wine facility and restaurant. It seems appropriate that this town, named for George C. Yount, who planted the first Napa Valley grape rootstock in 1838, would be home to another innovation—the first French-owned California winery.

Moët-Hennessey–Louis Vuitton is today's name for the massive French holding company that took a chance in 1973 and purchased vineyard land in three Napa Valley areas—Yountville, the Mount Veeder hills, and Carneros. The goal of the company and master winemaker Edmund Maudière was to grow Chardonnay, Pinot Noir, and Pinot Blanc grapes for sparkling-wine production. Simultaneously, the company decided to open a restaurant of high caliber where the sparkling wines, as well as other Napa Valley still wines, would be presented in an ideal setting for food and wine. None of the dedication to excellence has decreased at the stone-and-cement contemporary-style hospitality center and winery since its 1977 opening.

Near the landscaped entry road, an abstract fountain plays in one of the man-made ponds. Across the wooden footbridge is an underground hub of tourist activity. There you will find a well-designed display on cooperage (barrel making) and one on glass bottle making that includes an excellent visual on the various sizes of Champagne bottles, from the 187-milliliter smallest to the fifteen-liter Nebuchadnezzar. Some visitors walk up the interior cement steps and head for the restaurant; others choose to go directly to the salon at the head of the stairs, where they can sit at tables and purchase sparkling wine and appetizers. The majority of tourists congregate downstairs for the half-hour walking tour of the winery. Although the Grand Central Station noise level tends to mask the tour guide's opening remarks, the basic elements of the tour are friendly, educational, and performed with style. Tour groups are large here—thirty to forty visitors—but the guides have an unintimidating manner that invites questions from novices and experts. Photography is encouraged. Expect a good number of steps on this tour, as the facilities are built on different levels.

There is a thrill similar to discovering a secret in walking

the area lined with rows of 14,000 gallon stainless steel fermentation tanks. Eloquent guides such as Ellen Flora describe the *méthode champenoise* procedure of in-bottle fermentation, assisted by clear graphics, which demonstrate the movement of the dead yeast sediment. This yeast collects in the bottle and then is manipulated by riddling down into the bottle's neck for easy removal. In the riddling area, to which you descend, 200,000 bottles of wine rest their necks in wooden riddling racks, waiting silently for daily quarter-turns.

Within the Napa Valley, there is some confusion concerning the naming of sparkling wines. Some wineries call it Champagne; others dub it Napa Valley Champagne; and "sparkling wine" is used by many. Actually, all forms of nomenclature are legally correct. The Treaty of Madrid stated that only sparkling wine from the Champagne region of France could be called "Champagne." European countries signed the agreement in 1890, and as a result, Spain calls its sparkling wine *cava*, Italy calls it *spumanti*, and Germany names it *secht*. However, the United States never signed, on the principle that our "don't tread on me" attitude should not yield to such a dictate from Europe. Also, the later experience of Prohibition made the concept of sparkling wine produced in this country unthinkable. In any case, Domaine Chandon defers to the treaty's ruling because of the company's French parentage. Ergo, this sparkling wine is called just that.

To keep up with the high volume production of Domaine Chandon's Brut, Blanc de Noirs, Reserve, Première, Etoile, and Club Cuvée sparkling styles, very large machines (amusingly called VLMs) riddle hundreds of bottles simultaneously, creating the same small beads (bubbles) as the hand-riddled wine.

"Is it true," asks a tourist, "that the larger the bubbles the larger the headache?" The guide responds that large beads are called toad's eyes and that she believes there is some truth to the tale, although it has not been proven. She is quick to point out that the froth of bubbles atop a freshly poured glass of sparkling wine is called a mousse and not a head. "That's another beverage," she states with a smile.

Back upstairs you'll view the entire final wine-processing system from an upper platform. The stages of activity are well marked, so that the process is clear, even at the noisy peak of disgorging, corking, and bottle-tumbling to final foiling, labeling, and boxing of the bottles.

Given a dormant bottling line, the tour guide will use the quiet platform area to demonstrate how to properly open a bottle of sparkling wine. Basic information is given, such as, "Chill it three hours in the refrigerator or at least forty minutes in an ice bucket," as well as sparkling wine trivia: the speed at which a cork exits the bottle (sixty-two miles per hour) and how many counterclockwise turns will release the wire cage on any sparkling wine bottle in the world (six and one-half).

Good-byes are said alongside the Beaujolais horizontal-style press, which was used from 1600 through the late 1800s. Appropriately, the press is mounted near an imposing modern stone arch.

Without question, this winery blends the old and the new with strong touches of education and hospitality.

Freemark Abbey Winery

3022 St. Helena Highway
St. Helena, CA 94574
(707) 963-9694
fax (707) 963-0554

Website: www.freemarkabbey.com
Email:
retailmgr@freemarkabbey.com
wineclub@freemarkabbey.com

Winemaker/Managing Partner:
Ted Edwards
Winery owner: Partnership

Access

Location: Approximately 2 miles
north of St. Helena, at Highway 29
and Lodi Lane.

Hours open for visits and tastings:
May–October 10 A.M.–5 P.M.,
November–April 10 A.M.–4:30
P.M. Tours daily at 2 P.M.

Appointment necessary for tour?
Yes, for other than 2 P.M. tour.

Wheelchairs accommodated? Yes.

Tastings

Charge for tasting with tour? $4.
Tasting fee includes logo glass.

Charge for tasting without tour?
As above.

Typical wines offered: Four to five
current release wines, typically two
whites and three reds.

Sales of wine-related items? Yes.

Picnics and Programs

Picnic area open to the public?
No, private functions only.

Special events or wine-related
programs? Not regularly scheduled,
but winery does host private wine
dinners.

Just north of St. Helena, Freemark Abbey offers tourists the quiet blend of a century-old stone winery and a modern wine tasting room. Winter is my favorite season to visit this winery, due to the warm homecoming feeling evoked by the roaring fire in the stone fireplace and the living-room quality of the tasting room. There's a grand piano in a corner of the room, just beyond the fringes of an oriental carpet, and comfortable armchairs and sofas beckon to the traveler.

Freemark Abbey traces its origins to 1886 and to Josephine Tychson, the first woman to build and operate a California winery. During the tour you'll hear about her struggles as a young widow managing the vineyards and overseeing the original wooden winery. In 1898, St. Helena mayor Anton Forni bought Freemark Abbey. He built the native quarry stone structure using Chinese workers whose pickax marks are still visible on stones inside the winery.

A side note: if the Victorian-era history of the area fascinates you, don't miss the Sharpsteen Museum on Washington Street in Calistoga. There you'll see dioramas and exact representations of the town as it was when well-to-do San Franciscans traveled by ferry to Vallejo and then by train to Calistoga, where they bathed in the famous restorative mineral waters of the region. The museum includes photos of the "China camp" where laborers lived in community.

Albert Ahern, the winery's next owner, gave Freemark Abbey its name. Despite the seeming monastic style of its title, the winery's name actually derives from Ahern's nickname, Abbey, and a bit of each of the names of his two partners Charles Freeman and Mark Foster.

Today, the guided winery tour winds through the French doors of the tasting room onto a terrace with a view of the gardens and lawn fronting the original winery. As you walk along the vineyards and then down a gentle slope to view the crush pad area, the guide will explain that in 1966 Chuck Carpy, a grape grower and native St. Helenan, partnered with renowned vineyard manager Laurie Wood and five other men who were active in the community. That group worked to renovate Freemark Abbey, which had been relatively dormant for years. In the early nineties, Chuck Carpy, who has since died, told me, "The first thing we had to do was completely renovate the lower cellars. There were dirt floors, some dirt walls, and the cooperage was shot. Most of the old casks were pre-Prohibition." A year later, in 1967, Carpy and company brought in their first vintage.

Be sure to wear sweaters in the cellars—the two-foot-thick walls keep the temperature at fifty-five degrees, plus or minus one or two degrees, ideal for storing wine. While in the cellar you'll learn how to decipher the winemaker's cryptic notes on the sixty-gallon French and American oak barrels. You'll also probably meet the cellarmaster, Rene Estevez, unless the harvest, which yields around 40,000 cases of wine, is at its peak.

There are a candle shop and a couple of restaurants at the winery entrance, which can make this a full afternoon stop.

Grgich Hills Cellars

1829 St. Helena Highway
Rutherford, CA 94573
(707) 963-2784
fax (707) 963-8724
No website or email.

Winemaker: Miljenko "Mike" Grgich
Winery owners: Miljenko "Mike" Grgich and Austin Hills

Access

Location: On Highway 29, ½ mile north of Rutherford, on the west side of the highway.

Hours open for visits and tastings: 9:30 A.M.–4:30 P.M. daily, except Easter, Good Friday (half day), Thanksgiving, Christmas, and New Year's Day.

Appointment necessary for tour? Yes; check winery for times of the two tours a day, A.M. and P.M.

Wheelchairs accommodated? Yes.

Tastings

Charge for tasting with tour? On weekends and holidays only; $3 for each glass, not deductible from price of purchased wine.

Charge for tasting without tour? As above.

Typical wines offered: Chardonnay, Fumé Blanc, Zinfandel, Cabernet Sauvignon, and late harvest "Violetta."

Sales of wine-related items? Yes.

Picnics and Programs
Picnic area open to the public? No.

Special events or wine-related programs? The Pre-Release Club, which entitles members to early notification of new wines and also an annual festival. Discounts on wines through the club.

A t a time when U.S. wine marketing is based generally on wine with food, Miljenko "Mike" Grgich is a man whose winery is doing something specific about it.

The tour at Grgich Hills Cellars begins and ends with discussion of the link between wine making and food preparation, with specific examples to show the similarities. Take chicken stock. At home, you can make a delicious stock by combining essential base ingredients—at least chicken, onion, carrots, celery, and salt—in a pot with water, bringing it to a boil and then letting the rich flavors steep into the liquid during a slow simmer. You skim fats and residues that float to the surface or, for further refining, you can stir foamy egg whites into the broth as a "food magnet" to attract and hold tiny food particles. A fine sieve can then remove those impurities.

While standing in the award-bedecked tasting room, the knowledgeable Grgich guide explains how wine making is a similar series of activities. By combining flavor bases—grapes from various vineyards picked at different times and temperatures—and allowing the grapes to sit together, you induce fermentation and a cap of residue forms. The cap is then strained off and the fermented grape juice is refined, often with the help of egg whites, and bottled as wine, one of the few living, breathing, fermenting beverages.

"Wine is a living thing," the tour guide explains. "It will change over time because it is alive. Not so for spirits, which will never change."

The tour moves from the overly dark tasting room into the day's brilliance back at the winery's entry, and on to the edge of one of the early Grgich Hills vineyards paralleling Highway 29. There you'll learn that all the grapes are picked by hand, a dictate from Mike Grgich. Grgich is also the winemaker, having immigrated from Croatia with a strong desire to make wine; Austin Hills, the winery's co-owner, is an heir to the Hills Brothers coffee fortune. Hills jumped at the chance of partnership with Grgich immediately after the 1976 Paris "crowning" of the '76 Chateau Montelena Chardonnay, when he was winemaker there. Grgich had taken enology studies at the University of Zagreb and still wears a student beret.

As a winery to visit, Grgich Hills is ideal for connoisseurs and for those who wish to learn about wine making. You'll learn such tips as how to differentiate American oak barrels from French ones (American barrels have a narrow belly compared to the French, which can hold as much as 3.3 gallons more wine).

Why use oak barrels? The guide will explain that there's a biochemical interchange of phenol from the oak into the aging wine, which adds more flavor to the final product.

During a walk through the wine-making facility, you may see a number of cold-stabilization tanks jacketed in ice. Grgich, who follows classic wine-making techniques, filters his wines using this increasingly popular method of refining the fermented juice. Racking is another preferred technique that removes the depleted yeast and grape solids gently, resulting in a more "natural" wine. The wine tasting conducted for the tour takes place separated from the interior tasting room. On a sunny day, you'll sit outside in leafy shade under the trees or the redwood trellis. Only the hum of traffic on Highway 29 will distract as you and the other guests in your group sip Napa Valley Chardonnay, late harvest Johannisberg Riesling, and other varietals while learning how to taste wine and how to compare vintages.

Chances are you'll see Mike Grgich as you travel around the winery—watch for the man in a beret. If he is able to put his projects on hold, he'll happily answer your wine-making questions, adding to the wealth of understanding you will have gained from the tour.

The Hess Collection Winery

4411 Redwood Road
Napa, CA 94558
(707) 255-1144
fax (707) 253-1682
Website: www.hesscollection.com
Email: See website

Winemaker: Dave Guffy
Winery owner: Donald Hess

Access

Location: Going north on Highway 29 to the town of Napa, stay in the left-hand lane; turn left on Redwood Road at its intersection with Trancas. Continue west about 6 miles to the winery.

Hours open for visits and tastings: 10 A.M.–4 P.M. daily, except Easter, Thanksgiving, Christmas, and New Year's Day.

Appointment necessary for tour? No; for groups of 10 or more, call for reservation.

Wheelchairs accommodated? Yes.

Tastings

Charge for tasting with tour? $3, not deductible from price of purchased wine.

Charge for tasting without tour? As above.

Typical wines offered: Current releases of Chardonnay and Cabernet Sauvignon.

Sales of wine-related items? Yes, including museum catalog.

Picnics and Programs

Picnic area open to the public? No.

Special events or wine-related programs? Private dinners for up to 100 people.

Redwood Road winds along the southwestern hills of Napa, leading you through shaded forests of sequoias and fields of mountain wildflowers. Solitary hawks glide effortlessly, dotting clear blue skies with their graceful form. There is a subtle similarity here to driving circuitous routes in the Sierra foothills. Without question, this road is Northern California at its best.

With such a dramatic approach as Redwood Road leading to the Hess Collection Winery and museum, you might predict a lesser experience at road's end. But the truth is that the adventure only advances.

Walking from the parking area to the winery, you'll pass a sculpture garden and then face two splendid stone structures, merged with an internal spine of clean, contemporary architecture. The main building was constructed around 1903 as Mount La Salle, home for Northern California Christian Brothers. Once inside, you'll experience airy spaciousness. There is a mix of early-twentieth-century stonework and quiet modern lines that acts as a background for art and a stage for winery procedures.

The gratis tour here is self-guided and incorporates elements of the art of wine making with a museum of contemporary paintings and sculptures that are mounted in a thirteen-thousand-square-foot gallery. Visitors have the opportunity to view works by Frank Stella, Magdalena Abakanowicz, Francis Bacon, and other world-renowned artists. This museum is winery owner Donald Hess's "gift to the public." Hess is a Swiss-American ninth-generation brewmaster based in Bern. There he headquarters a variety of companies including Valser St. Petersquelle, the second-largest brand of mineral water in Switzerland; an alpine trout hatchery; and eighteen restaurants.

Hess believed that his vineyards, winery, and museum would fare well on Mount Veeder, an extinct volcano in the Mayacamas range, due to the stress of surviving in the rocky soil of the Mount Veeder appellation. He had good reason. Although a visit to the hilly vineyards is not possible, they can be viewed in two ways: stop at one of the gallery's dormer windows and glance at the promontory across the way. You may see workers pruning the vines. Or take a few minutes to view the nine-projector slide show in the small theater on the winery's second floor. The seats are as comfortable as the plushest theater accommodation, and the room is a cool respite on a scorching day.

The slide presentation is the finest of any I have seen in the industry. The images take you through the 130-day push in the grape growing cycle. Pictures and music highlight seasonal changes while they introduce the people, techniques, and equipment necessary to make fine wine.

On exiting the theater, you can't miss Leopold Malers' *Hommage 1974*, a flaming typewriter with a powerful image.

After the self-guided tour (with easy access by stairway or elevator), you will pass the massive floral arrangement on the first floor and proceed to the tasting room. There you'll find a huge wooden bar in a room surrounded by stone walls and aging barrels. The room's warm tones contrast with the gallery's brightness. The hosts and hostesses can answer any wine-making or tasting questions about the winery's Cabernet Sauvignons and Chardonnays.

My guess is that this winery visit will be one of the most memorable of your Napa Valley tour.

Charles Krug Winery

2800 Main Street
St. Helena, CA 94574
(707) 963-5057
fax (707) 963-7913
Website: None
Email: charleskrug@pmondavi.com

Winemaker: Jac Cole

Winery owners: Peter Mondavi, Sr.;
Peter Mondavi, Jr.; Marc Mondavi

Access

Location: On Highway 29 north of
St. Helena; on the road's northeast
side between the "tunnel of elms"
and Deer Park Road.

Hours open for visits and tastings:
10 A.M.–5 P.M. daily, except all
Wednesdays, Easter, Thanksgiving,
Christmas Eve, Christmas, and New
Year's Day.

Appointment necessary for tour? No.

Wheelchairs accommodated? Yes.

Tastings

Charge for tasting with tour? $3.

Charge for tasting without tour?
$3 for four wines, $5 for four
Vintage Selection or Family Reserve.

Typical wines offered: Cabernet
Sauvignon, Merlot, Chardonnay,
Sangiovese, Pinot Noir, and other
varietals.

Sales of wine-related items?
Yes, a wide variety.

Picnics and Programs

Picnic area open to the public? No.

Special events or wine-related
programs? An annual series of
invitational "Tastings on the Lawn."
New releases are offered with cheese
and music. For information about
special events, call 800-747-5784.

One of the best vineyard tours in the Napa Valley is offered at the Charles Krug Winery. Actually, this should be the case, considering the fact that Krug, founded in 1861, is the oldest winery in the valley. Numerous excellent winemakers have apprenticed and worked in the twelve-hundred-acre vineyard, and the tradition of reverence for the land is apparent during the tour.

On a midweek afternoon, you can expect to share the vineyard and production facility tour with people from all over the world, as the wine has international recognition.

A favorite time of year to visit the winery is late spring, when mustard flowers make the approach to the winery a sea of yellow blossoms and dogwoods add pink and white touches along distant hills, where Mount St. Helena, a formerly active volcano to the north, rises 4,300 feet above the pastel valley floor. From the parking area looking west, there is also an outstanding view of Greystone Cellars, the imposing stone building that earlier housed The Christian Brothers wine cellars. Now that structure is the new home of the Culinary Institute of America Center for Continuing Education.

Considering the history and glamour of Charles Krug Winery's past, the welcoming area is friendly in an understated way. But the true reason to tour this winery is to learn the stages of the life of wine grapes from the vineyard point of view. Knowledgeable tour guides use down-to-earth language in describing such stages as "bud break" (the first sign of buds in spring), "veraison" (grape skin coloration), and "brix" (sugar level of grapes).

"Bud break," explained one Charles Krug guide, "happens when the soil temperature is between fifty and fifty-five degrees. Then leaves and flower buds are growing about one inch a week—like a kid with a haircut."

The relatively small number of tourists on the guided walk is a boon when you're walking right into the vineyards. The tour guide is easily heard as he discusses trellising systems for grapevines. During the outdoor visit, the guide will point out that "cordons" are two canes or "arms" that are left to trail from the main trunk of the vine, as opposed to the "kicker cane," which is one cane left from the past year's growth.

Questions are encouraged, no matter how basic. Want to see smudge pots (portable agricultural gas heaters)? No problem—the group moves over to view them, at the request. You'll walk through the production area as well, viewing fermentation tanks and barrels. Since the winery makes fourteen varietals, ranging from White Zinfandel to vintage-selection

Cabernet Sauvignon, some activity is bound to be taking place, no matter what season of the year.

The winery has a rich history, which is discussed at the long wooden tasting bar while at least three wines are offered. It was Charles Krug who founded the winery and was a moving force in the infant Napa Valley wine industry, encouraging some of his assistant winemakers, such as Jacob Beringer, to move out on their own to strengthen the business. Krug was the first in the valley to use a wine press, rather than the foot-stomping method employed until then. When Krug died, in 1902, a friend held the winery in receivership until Cesare Mondavi brought it back to life in 1943. It was from this winery that Robert Mondavi moved to found his own company. And the Charles Krug Winery is still owned and operated by Cesare's son Peter Mondavi and by his sons, Marc and Peter, Jr.

Although the old family home is not open to the public, Krug's hospitality is offered throughout the year during the Harvest Festival and a variety of music performances.

LOUIS M. MARTINI WINERY

Louis M. Martini Winery

254 South St. Helena Highway
St. Helena, CA 94574
(707) 963-2736
fax (707) 963-8750

Website: www.louismartini.com

Winemaker: Michael Martini

Winery owner: The Martini family

Access

Location: South of the St. Helena city limits on the northeast side of Highway 29.

Hours open for visits and tastings: 10 A.M.–4:30 P.M. daily, except Easter, Thanksgiving, Christmas Eve, Christmas, and New Year's Day. Tours given continuously.

Appointment necessary for tour? No.

Wheelchairs accommodated? Yes.

Tastings

Charge for tasting with tour? No.

Charge for tasting without tour? No, except that five reserve wines may be tasted for $5 (includes logo glass); not deductible from price of purchased wine.

Typical wines offered: Varies each month; usually six each day, featuring a Cabernet and a Chardonnay.

Sales of wine-related items? Yes.

Picnics and Programs

Picnic area open to the public? Yes.

Special events or wine-related programs? Yes.

Of all the wineries chosen for this collection, the Louis M. Martini Winery in St. Helena may be the least imposing in appearance. Yet considering the family tradition and the longtime dedication by three generations of Martini winemakers, this establishment is well worth a visit.

The emphasis in the hospitality room is on two walls: one wall is hung with historical and agricultural photos; the facing wall houses a long wooden wine bar. Wine production is the family story, and the tastings are extensive. Six wines are offered as a daily complimentary tasting, including older, twelve- to eighteen-year-old wines. For a minimal fee you can also taste the winery's reserve wines.

Few wineries in the valley have inventory enough to be able to share such a varied selection of older Zinfandels and Cabernet Sauvignons. But Martini can: the company, which was founded in 1922 by Louis M. Martini in Kingsburg, in the San Joaquin Valley, has consistently held back wine to share with visitors.

Oddly, the winery's first production came during Prohibition and so wasn't wine at all, but a grape concentrate for home wine making named "Forbidden Fruit." Now, with production of 150,000 cases of wine and a storage capacity of 2.1 million gallons, the library of older wines here is extremely comprehensive.

There is an open friendliness in the ambiance at Martini. Tourists are encouraged to bring a picnic lunch to enjoy with wine under the sycamore trees in the quiet of the back garden. Tables and benches are available all day in this hideaway garden, one of the Napa Valley secrets.

The winery tour gives a complete overview of the winemaking process, including a close-up of the crush during harvest. Since the family of Martini winemakers has a tradition of innovation, you will view a number of unusual machines that were derived or purchased to enhance the vintners' process over the years. I have heard tour guides say, "We call that the espresso machine," when pointing to a large stainless steel and iron centrifuge sporting wheels, spouts, and bulges.

The innovations from the Martinis actually have been considerable. Louis M. Martini was the first winemaker to purchase substantial acreage in the Carneros region for wine grape cultivation. The family also has developed vineyards in Sonoma Valley as well as the renowned Monte Rosso Vineyard in Lake County and other vineyards in the Chiles and Pope valleys in Napa County. Other innovations include Louis' improvements in grape varieties, changes that aided the industry considerably. He also pioneered mechanical harvesting in California, a method now used in about 65 percent of the vineyards.

There are beautiful old wooden doors to watch for as the guide covers the property from the visitors' center to the solera Sherry aging facility and back. Note the pyramid barrel stacks in the aging rooms. There is usually at least one in the tour group who recalls the huge redwood tanks that until recently nearly filled one massive room. When Louis M.'s grandson Michael accepted the responsibility of wine making from his father, Louis P. Martini, he decided to increase the use of sixty-gallon French oak barrels in order to age his wines. Then it was good-bye to the huge tanks of old.

Once back in the tasting room, you might notice the wooden structures around the skylights. They have a strong resemblance to the bases of wine presses; it's so typical of the Martini family to bring the direction right back to wine making.

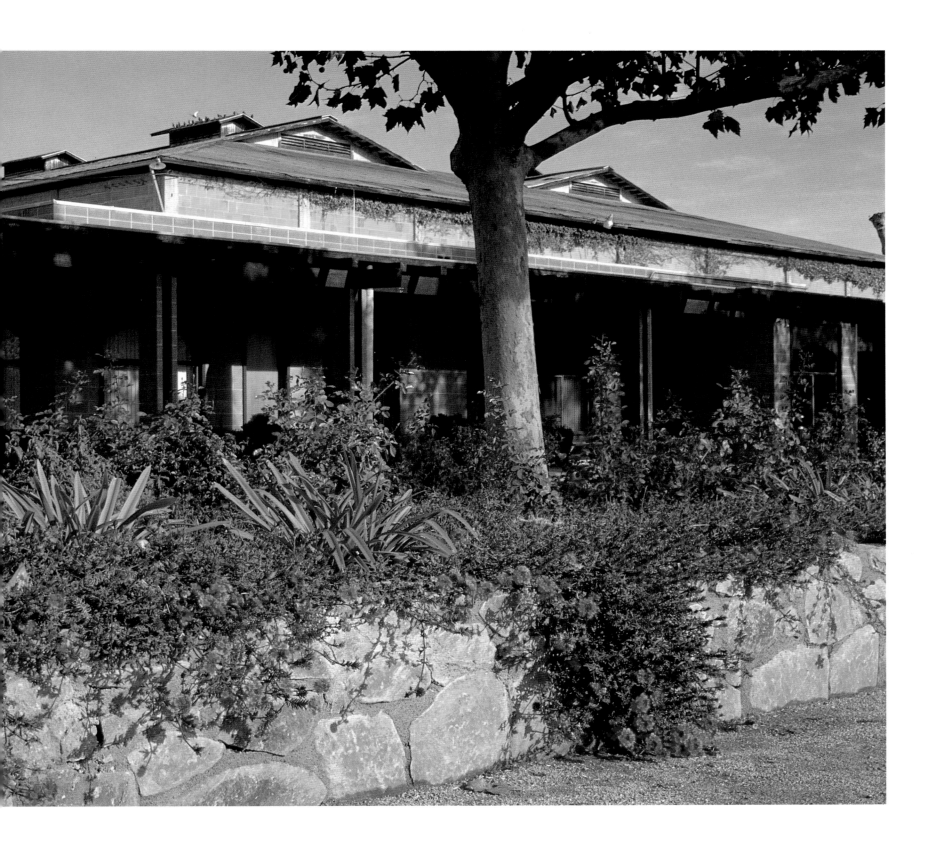

Robert Mondavi Winery

7801 St. Helena Highway
Oakville, CA 94562
(707) 963-9611
fax (707) 963-1007
Website: www.robertmondavi.com
Email: info@robertmondavi.com

Winemaker: Tim Mondavi
Winery owner:
The Robert Mondavi family

Access

Location: On Highway 29, ⅛ mile
north of Oakville.

Hours open for visits and tastings:
9 A.M.–5:30 P.M. May–October,
9:30 A.M.–4:30 P.M. November–
April, except Thanksgiving,
Christmas, and New Year's Day.

Appointment necessary for tour?
Yes, suggested; preferably in
advance, but sometimes available
the same day.

Wheelchairs accommodated? Yes.

Tastings

Charge for tasting with tour? No.

Charge for tasting without tour? Per
glass; prices vary.

Typical wines offered: Current
vintages of Chardonnay, Cabernet
Sauvignon, Fumé Blanc, Moscato
d'Oro, Pinot Noir. In the reserve
tasting area, as featured by the taste.

Sales of wine-related items? Yes,
including logo glasses ($3.95 for
4 ½ oz. and $6.95 for 11 ½ oz.).

Picnics and Programs

Picnic area open to the public? No.

Special events or wine-related
programs? The Robert Mondavi
Summer Jazz Festival, The Great
Chefs Program (a series of cooking
classes and meals taught/cooked by
noted culinary stars; open to the
public), Wine of the Month program,
and the Human Race, a vineyard run.

The entrance to the Robert Mondavi Winery in Oakville is a generous one, much like the spirit of its founder, who has tirelessly led the California wine industry since he founded his family company in 1966. Broad steps lead past a sleek granite bear sculpted by Beniamino Bufano, and as you approach the terrace the massive mission-style arch frames a splendid vista of the western vineyards and hills.

To many who make the pilgrimage to the valley, the Robert Mondavi Winery is mecca, and their hopes of learning about wine are answered here at the winery known, above all others in the Napa Valley, for its excellent tours.

"Let me say that there are as many different wines as there are types of bread or fish in the sea," notes tour guide Kurt Cobbett as he leads a group of twenty-five guests from the visitors' center into the vineyard facing the parking lot. With that opener, Kurt sets the two themes that are clearly elemental to the Robert Mondavi family philosophy: education leads to knowledge and enjoyment, and wine is a natural accompaniment to food.

If you tour during the late summer and at harvest time you'll be encouraged to sample some of the Sauvignon Blanc grapes from the front vineyard, where some discussion on the history of wine will take place. For instance, wine has its roots in the Middle East, where wine vessels dating to 7000 B.C. have been discovered.

It's no wonder why grapes thrive in the dry desertlike climate of the Napa Valley, where rainfall is typically absent from April through November.

Moving from the vineyard to the crush pad, guests learn that the stemmer-crusher, which looks like a giant cheese grater, is used to separate grapes from their stems before crushing them. Seemingly small details are added during the discussion, such as the tip that Pinot Noir stems are allowed to remain with the grape, whereas Cabernet Sauvignon stems are removed. If you took notes during a Robert Mondavi tour, you could almost go home and make your own vintage; there are no secrets here.

Once inside a vast room lined with rows of huge steel vats, the guide explains fermentation as "nothing more than little yeast cells eating grape juice." He likens the steel tanks to the pots and pans in your kitchen: airtight, because air can spoil food or wine; easily cleaned, and able to take refrigeration.

"How can a red grape give white wine?" asks one tourist. I've heard Kurt, as well as other Robert Mondavi tour guides, answer by referring to a different fruit: "Think of an apple. It has red skin, white fruit, and clear juice, just like a grape. If we want white wine, we squeeze the juice and remove the skins.

"If we want to make red wine, we would leave the skins in with the juice for a certain amount of time and then press the mixture and strain off the skins."

Due to the simplified explanations of the ancient art of wine making, you can finally understand the basic process and see other heads nodding as you walk to the barrel aging area. The tour guide continues to demystify wine making while reviewing serious numbers, such as the fact that the winery holds 45,000 small French oak barrels. Since each sixty-gallon barrel costs $600, barrels come second only to farming costs in winery expenses.

One of the tour's most pleasant walks follows the visit to the technical wine-making wing of the operation. Tourists stroll around the renowned To-Kalon vineyard bordered by rosebushes. The $27 million To-Kalon renovation project will result in a new state-of-the-art facility for producing and barrel-aging the winery's high-end reds as well as improvements to the winery visitors' programs.

The extensive manicured lawn at Mondavi stretches toward the entry; this lawn is the scene of summer evening jazz concerts during which the winery has presented such greats as Ella Fitzgerald and Ray Charles, while visitors picnic on the green. Following the terra-cotta tiles along the lawn's curve, you'll pass the Vineyard Room off the hospitality wing. There the Mondavi family, under the guidance of Margrit Biever (Robert Mondavi's wife), hosts art shows, concerts, and literary presentations in conjunction with its mission to link wine appreciation with recognition of all the arts.

Your group will conclude its tour with an extensive tasting, which once again promotes education along with enjoyment. You will settle in one of the small adobe tasting rooms or in a shaded area outside. The Mondavi tour guides share a word to the wise about wine tasting: "Just pretend you're eating a hamburger—look at it, smell it, and taste it. It's that simple."

During the tasting, questions and observations are encouraged. When a question is posed on the color of red wine related to vintage, the guide places a white linen napkin over a plate and pours a '79 Cabernet Reserve beside an '82 and an '87 to discuss the differences. Aging causes a slightly brown tinge due to oxidation, which shows on the napkin. Younger wines usually yield a more intense color.

With its vigorous dedication to the marriage of food with wine, the winery has a full complement of chefs who prepare meals for special events. At this writing, Mondavi is one of the few wineries that offer a taste of food other than crackers or bread to complement a tour's wine tasting. As an example, small squares of a peach tart—and its recipe—are offered in tandem with Moscato d'Oro dessert wine.

The educational tour and taste program was initiated at the opening of the Robert Mondavi Winery, at a time when there were only twenty-six active wineries in the Napa Valley. Since then, nearly three hundred wineries have grown along Highway 29 and the Silverado Trail as well as on western and eastern slopes. Through all the expansion, this winery has been a central beacon to visitors, growers, and vintners.

MUMM NAPA VALLEY

Mumm Napa Valley

8445 Silverado Trail
Rutherford, CA 94573
(707) 942-3434
fax (707) 942-3470
Website: www.mumm.com
Email: concierge@sparkling.com

Winemakers: Greg Fowler,
Rob McNeill

Winery owner: Chateau & Estate
Wines Company

Access

Location: 5 minutes' drive south of
St. Helena on the Silverado Trail,
between Conn Creek Road (Highway
128) and Oakville Cross Road.

Hours open for visits and tastings:
10:30 A.M.–6 P.M. April through
October, 10 A.M.–5 P.M. November
through March. Tours on the hour
11 A.M.–4 P.M.

Appointment necessary? No.

Wheelchairs accommodated? Yes.

Tastings

Charge for tasting with tour? $3.75
a flute (full glass), not deductible
from price of purchased wine.

Charge for tasting without tour?
As above.

Typical wines offered: Mumm
Cuvée Napa, Brut Prestige, Blanc de
Noirs, Blanc de Blancs, Winery Lake
Cuvée, and limited releases avail-
able only at the winery.

Sales of wine-related items?
Yes, including $5 logo glass.

Picnics and Programs

Picnic area open to the public? No.

Special events or wine-related
programs? Wine Club, catered
luncheons, dinners, receptions, fine
art openings and permanent Ansel
Adams photography exhibit
entitled "The Story of a Winery."

A California plantation house. While you sit on the veranda at Mumm Napa Valley, sipping sparkling Blanc de Noirs and gazing westward over acres of Cabernet Sauvignon grapes, the image develops of a California-variety plantation. New-age flute music, white chairs, and creamy white Italian canvas umbrellas shading the sun's rays contrast with thriving green philodendron plants and verdigris metal chairs in the glass-enclosed exteriors of the hospitality center. Massive, *Casablanca*-style fans push soft breezes in the room while a young woman smiles and asks, "Sparkling wine or mineral water?"

This winery offers the California dream in contemporary style. Its facilities reveal wine-making equipment ranked among the most modern in the world.

Touring is easily done, all on one level, due to an excellent walkway system bordering the huge fermentation tanks. On autumn tours I have taken, the tour guides have been articulate, aware of the stages of the wine-making art, and sophisticated enough to relate to visitors from a variety of backgrounds. Three very short videos are presented during different points in the tour to demonstrate activities that occur only seasonally: the harvesting process, bottling, and disgorgement. In fact, in my opinion none of the tours and tour guides covered in this collection can rival those of Mumm Napa Valley, along with Robert Mondavi and St. Supéry, for comprehensive, visitor-friendly tours.

Your tour will depart from the visitors' center and proceed down a paved path to a mini-vineyard where Pinot Meunier, Chardonnay, Pinot Gris, and Pinot Noir grapes grow. Since the fruit used for actual production is grown "down valley" in the Carneros region, the small vineyard offers a practical demonstration of a year's cycle of grape growth. (The eighty acres of Cabernet Sauvignon vines surrounding the Mumm Napa Valley estate produce grapes to make Sterling wine. Sterling, Mumm Napa Valley, and Three Palms are all owned by Seagram Chateau & Estate Wines. G. H. Mumm et Cie of Reims, France, co-owns the Mumm Napa Valley venture.)

The tour guide is sure to mention that "although all Champagne is sparkling wine, not all sparkling wines are Champagne." Almost every guide at every sparkling winery makes the same statement.

There is little discussion as you pass the fermentation tanks arranged as neatly as steel tanks in the most modern dairy. The largest tank of all is centrally located in the vast room. As its 65,000-gallon capacity is described in one-bottle measure, if you drank one 750-milliliter bottle of wine a day, it would take 898 years to empty the vat.

At the walkway's end, there is an observation platform from which you'll see the arrival area for grapes during harvest. If you visit this or any winery during "the crush," as grape harvest is called, you'll see action. Workers are laboring six, sometimes seven days a week, twelve to fourteen hours per day. The fruit is delivered in bins as yellow as mustard on a hot dog.

Winemakers Greg Fowler and Rob McNeill both consulted with the late founder, Guy Devaux of France. They have chosen the classic method of treating grapes for sparkling wines: the stemmer-crusher is employed, because it is gentle on the grape skins. Rough handling would break the skins, releasing highly tannic seeds into the grape juice. "You want tannins in still wines," explains the tour guide, "but not in sparklers." When the just-crushed juice is siphoned into a tank, yeast is added immediately to help convert the juice's sugar into alcohol. This first fermentation method is identical to that of a still wine.

The difference in making sparkling wine in the *méthode champenoise* manner is that the wine is then funneled into heavy bottles, which are stopped with a small plastic *bidule* (translates from French as "thingamajig"), which acts as a plug. The bottles are then capped with a metal soda pop top. During the one-and-a-half to four years the bottles lie on their sides, ninety to a hundred pounds of pressure per square inch builds within each bottle. That's the same pressure as that of a car tire, applied to a wine bottle.

By now, you are in a wide corridor looking through windows at a variety of activities: to one side is the automatic riddling room where VLMs (very large machines) are stacked with pallets of filled bottles. The VLMs turn, every six hours, to encourage the sedimentary mass of dead yeast cells to collect at the bottle necks. On the other side of the corridor, you'll see the impeccable, large laboratory.

Look through yet another large window to view the freezing and disgorging treatments of the wine. Here, necks of bottles filled with aged, bottle-fermented wine are frozen automatically in a negative twenty-three degrees centigrade propylene glycol bath, followed by removal of the metal caps. This action forces the *bidules* and frozen plugs of yeast to burst from the bottles. The *dosage*—addition of a small amount of sugar—reduces acidity and "softens" the wine.

Finally, on to a viewing station above the bottling line, where a hundred thousand cases of sparkling wine annually receive their corks, wire cages over the corks, labels, and neck foils. The whole procedure is fully automated and moves with the precision of a music box with dancing figures.

There is a wall-mounted demonstration of how champagne corks are made, with layers of glued cork pressed into a mass that is then cut. The tour guide will field questions with ease, and will act as your waiter on returning to the visitors' center. There, for a change, you can enjoy generous tastings of the various sparkling wines as well as sweet or savory appetizers while being shaded by Italian umbrellas and lulled by the strains of flute music.

California, indeed.

Niebaum-Coppola Estate Winery

1991 St. Helena Highway
Rutherford, CA 94573
(707) 968-1100
fax (707) 967-3355
Website: www.niebaum-coppola.com
Email: None.

Winemaker: Scott McLeod
Winery owners:
Francis Ford and Eleanor Coppola

Access

Location: Highway 29, north of
Oakville in the town of Rutherford,
first left (to the east) after
Niebaum Lane.

Hours open for visits and tastings:
10 A.M.–5 P.M. daily, except
Easter, Thanksgiving, Christmas Eve,
Christmas Day, and New Year's Day.

Appointment necessary for tour?
Yes. Please call (707) 968-1161.

Wheelchairs accommodated? Yes.

Tastings

Charge for tasting with tour? Yes;
prices vary. One tour ($20) is
accompanied by a wine and cheese
tasting.

Charge for tasting without tour?
Yes; $7.50 includes four wines and
logo glass.

Typical wines offered: Wines vary
depending on availability.

Sales of wine-related items? Yes.

Picnics and Programs

Picnic area open to the public? No.

Special events or wine-related
programs? Call for information
about special events:
(707) 968-1100.

When you turn off Highway 29 onto the Rutherford property of the Niebaum-Coppola Estate Winery, imagine you're bouncing in a horse-drawn carriage down the one-fifth-mile entry drive.

The earth to your right and left has yielded wine grapes since Finnish fur trader Captain Gustave Niebaum founded this winery in 1879. As you alight from your "carriage," you'll become aware of a deep sense of dual traditions here. Ivy-covered winery buildings face a square as large as the hub of some European towns. The original stone winery lies to the west of a massive reflecting pool. The ninety-foot-long pool was added as part of major interior and exterior refurbishing of the property by Francis Ford and Eleanor Coppola, who are, since late 1994, the owners of this historic winery chateau and vineyard land in the heart of the Napa Valley.

The wine-making facility is a reminder of late-nineteenth-century Bordeaux-style architecture. The particularly interesting mix here is the fact that renowned film director Coppola has put his stamp inside the stone chateau, with such additions as flashy *Dracula* costumes, plans from the filming of *Apocalypse Now*, and the desk from the original set of *The Godfather*, all of which are housed on the second floor of the building. The result? A mesh of old and new traditions, both bent on pleasing the public with memorable sights and wines.

For a beautiful view, walk the gentle slope to the crest of the hill just south of the chateau. There you will find the original fountain that was hauled by slow flatbed truck to its new home. It presides there over a panorama of vineyards, olive trees, and the Victorian home once the domicile of Captain Niebaum, now the private home of the Coppolas.

By noting the building's fine details, you will understand why it was five years in construction, opening in 1879. To best appreciate the place, step over the original "Inglenook" embedded in the stone entry and walk around the entry hall to view the Captain's Room. More a museum than a hospitality center, the room resembles a ship's ward room, down to its porthole window, shelf railings, and latched cupboard doors. The room and entry hall house a four-hundred-year-old glass lamp and sixteenth-century Flemish wine cups and other valuable items. From there you will face the grand staircase enhanced by buttery wooden pedestals hand-carved from wood imported from Belize (where the Coppolas own a lavish resort).

To the right is a series of rooms including a well-stocked retail space, possibly the largest in a Napa Valley winery. Eleanor Coppola chooses most of the items, which range from *Apocalypse Now* T-shirts to berets to pasta, home-grown olive oil, and a variety of tableware and books. Adjacent is the wine-tasting room. The winery pours numerous wine varietals, offering a chance to zero in on elegant vintages or wines for more relaxed dining. A tour with wine and cheese tasting is available; at $20 per person, it is the most expensive tour in the valley.

Keep your eyes open as you walk upstairs and you'll spy an original Tucker (an auto featured in Coppola's film of the same name). Look to one side of the automobile and you'll see five Oscars amassed by the Coppolas over the years. Behind the stairs, see a glass-encased Niebaum and Inglenook and Coppola memorabilia collection that evokes the inevitable sense of living with history, once again demonstrating the two sides of tradition awaiting the winery visitor.

Another find is the extensive wine library to the left of the main entrance. The bottle collection houses Inglenook vintages dating back to 1887. Although ancient vintages are not available for public tasting, they are occasionally offered for extraordinary auctions or wine industry tastings.

During your stay at the winery, you will probably learn about the typical Napa Valley soil so important to the success of the wines. Ask any guide for information on the earth in this Rutherford region. You will find that it is rocky, well-drained, and alluvial. The first layer of soil typical in the Napa Valley, also called the top layer of "plowed pan," contains dark humus and the blue-gray Bale Clay, mixed together. History states that when Captain Niebaum bought the property, he diverted the stream to the north, but the underlying sandy and gravelly sediments from the meandering stream remain, yielding alluvial soil. Sandstone gravels and highly colored chert pebbles eroded from the third layer. Chert, created as a result of high heat, proves past volcanic activity in the area. The fourth layer is an interface of cobbles incorporated with clay, and the base is bedrock. It is important to understand that poor, rocky soil requires roots to stretch and to hold it during their typically thirty-year life span.

An explanation of the soil sheds light on answers to two frequent questions concerning vineyard management:

How often do you water the vines? Rarely, if at all. Roots seek out the water level, which is twenty to thirty feet below the surface. However, vineyard managers often install a drip irrigation system to handle overly dry soil during times of drought and extreme heat.

Do you uproot the vines frequently? There are some vines here in the Napa Valley that have survived for well over fifty years. For example, Trefethen, Beringer, and Niebaum-Coppola are a few vineyards with some rootstock of that age or older. The vines still bear fruit. In the Napa Valley, rootstock remains planted thirty years on average, unless there is a plant disease.

Real wine-making history was made by Captain Niebaum's great-nephew, John Daniel, Jr., during the thirty years he headed Inglenook, from 1934 to 1964. Among other giant strides, Daniel promoted and gained acceptance for the Napa Valley appellation, pioneered vintage-dating of wines, and pushed for varietal designations for wines from the region, all steps toward solidifying the valley as a home of great wines.

What else is in store for the chateau? Francis Coppola says that there will be a film museum in the future. Other plans might include a more prominent placement of the *Apocalypse Now* camouflage boat that rests in dry dock on the property. But these ideas are just the tip of Coppola's hopes for the future of the winery. Who knows what "Gustave's Godfather" will dream next?

Joseph Phelps
Vineyards

200 Taplin Road
St. Helena, CA 94574
(707) 963-2745
fax (707) 963-4831
Website: www.jpvwines.com
Email: jpvwines@aol.com

Winemaker: Craig Williams
Winery owner: Joseph Phelps

Access

Location: On the Silverado Trail
driving north, 2 miles north of
Zinfandel Lane, turn onto Taplin
Road—it's the first winery on the
left.

Hours open for visits and tastings:
Tours: Monday–Friday 11 A.M.,
1 P.M. and 3 P.M.; Saturday 10
A.M., 11:30 A.M., 1 P.M. and 3
P.M.; Sunday 11 A.M., 1 P.M. and
2:30 P.M.

Appointment necessary for tours? Yes;
all tours and tastings are by appointment only.

Wheelchairs accommodated? Yes.

Tastings
Charge for tasting with tour? $3.

Charge for tasting without tour?
As above.

Typical wines offered: Those
currently available—usually
four—including Cabernet
Sauvignon and Chardonnay.

Sales of wine-related items? Yes.

Picnics and Programs
Picnic area open to the public?
Yes, though not always available;
request permission in advance.

Special events or wine-related
programs? No

The forest green Spring Valley schoolhouse at Taplin Road along the Silverado Trail is a showstopper. The century-old school sits unchanged in a woodsy glen, marking the entrance to Joseph Phelps Vineyards property where you'll find one of the truly spectacular views in the valley, particularly at springtime. Drive up Taplin to the imposing gateway crafted from redwood bridge timbers. Once on Phelps' land, you may feel a sense of the Napa Valley as it was at the turn of the century. The reason for this hindsight vision is that Joe Phelps planted grape rootstock on only 175 acres of the former Connolly Hereford Ranch, thus maintaining rolling hills and erratic hillocks through-out 600 acres of prime land, much as it was when visits to neighboring ranches were by horse and buggy.

Phelps, who came to the valley with a background as a

contractor, is typical of those who visited and decided to remain. During the late 1960s, he was hired to build two Souverain wineries, then owned by the Pillsbury Company. Today those wineries are Rutherford Hill in the Napa Valley and Chateau Souverain in the Alexander Valley. As a result of those experiences, he purchased this property for his own winery, which he built in a big-timber, Colorado style. Massive redwood beams mesh with steel and glass, giving a feeling of solid new tradition built to last the test of time.

If you arrive in the spring, masses of pale violet wisteria will be draping the redwood timbers that bridge the winery's two pavilions—one housing the steel fermentation tanks and some small oak tanks, and the other housing the barrels made of French oak for aging Cabernets, Chardonnays, and other wines. In this pavilion, you'll also find Yugoslavian oak used, because Yugoslavian oak does not impart flavors to Sauvignon Blancs and Gewürztraminers. The wisteria hints at the beautiful flower beds awaiting the visitors, particularly those viewed while looking down the vineyard from the back patio.

Each time I've toured Phelps Vineyards, two distinct characteristics about the visitors have manifested themselves: first, many guests are true flower fanciers and come to view the plantings, and second, the tourists seem to be a fun-loving group. There is no explaining this latter enthusiastic spirit, unless it is the joie de vivre of the cheerful tour guides at the winery.

The tour commences on the patio in fair weather, or on the oriental carpet in the winery's foyer. There, visitors learn that this one winery produces twenty-five different varietal wines with a bottling of only 100,000 cases, a relatively small production for most wineries that have land holdings of four hundred acres (Phelps also owns vineyards in Oakville, Rutherford, Yountville, Stags Leap, and Carneros in Napa Valley, as well as in King City in Monterey County).

Despite the quiet panorama from the patio, there is furious activity at the Taplin Road winery property and much for wine fanciers to learn. Phelps exemplifies the use of stainless steel for fermentation, and it was at this winery that the true Syrah grape of France's Rhone Valley was first bottled in California, as opposed to the state's more recognized Petite Syrah.

After visiting the 3,500 barrels in the cool fermentation chambers, a tasting under the patio arbor is perfectly timed. You'll taste at least four wines, perhaps more, depending on the tour guide and the time of day. The shaded picnic area, which must be reserved ahead, is an ideal nook above the vineyards.

In fact, you could plan a complete Joseph Phelps–inspired outing: call ahead to reserve a tour and request a table at the Phelps picnic area, then shop at the Oakville Grocery on Highway 29 at Oakville Crossroad (the picnic-perfect grocery is one of Phelps's projects; it houses an array of cheeses, breads, wine, pastries, and international goodies). With your basket filled, head for "the Trail" and Taplin Road in time for your tour and then settle down for a relaxed outdoor meal with wine from the source. Such a day, wrapped in memories of wisteria and wine, will long be remembered.

Rutherford Hill Winery

200 Rutherford Hill Road
Rutherford, CA 94573
(707) 963-1871
fax (707) 963-1878
Website: www.rutherfordhill.com
Email: info@rutherfordhill.com

Winemakers: Kevin Robinson,
Kent Barthman
Winery owners: Anthony, William,
and John Terlato

Access

Location: On the Silverado Trail, just
north of the Rutherford crossroad,
turn onto Rutherford Hill Road.
(Look for the large inscribed rock.)

Hours open for visits and tastings:
10 A.M.–4:30 P.M. daily, except
Thanksgiving, Christmas, and New
Year's Day.

Appointment necessary for tour? No.

Wheelchairs accommodated? Yes.

Tastings

Charge for tasting with tour? $4
includes logo glass, not deductible
from price of purchased wine.

Charge for tasting without tour?
As above.

Typical wines offered: Three
varietals, including Merlot,
Chardonnay, Cabernet Sauvignon,
and often Gewürztraminer or
Sauvignon Blanc.

Sales of wine-related items? Yes.

Picnics and Programs

Picnic area open to the public?
Yes, reserved for winery customers.

Special events or wine-related
programs: The Rutherford Hill Club,
includes pre-release announce-
ments, picnic table reservations,
and special events.

Spelunkers, take notice: there are 36,000 square feet of caves in the eastern Napa Valley foothills above Rutherford Hill Winery. The cave system, which is 120 feet below ground in some areas, is one of the largest created for wine aging in North America. It was dug mechanically under the direction of Alf Bertleson during the 1980s and is secured with a gunite surface.

So, what does an extensive cave system have to do with Rutherford Hill wine, or any wine, for that matter? The use of caves for wine storage is an ancient tradition. The French word for cellar is *cave*, and we English-speakers have adopted the word to mean a cavern or hollowed-out chamber of earth. Historically, wines have been aged in caves because the temperature within the earth is often as low as or lower than the fifty to sixty degrees ideal for a slow, even fermentation of grape juice. Also, the humidity within caves is a constant 90 percent, reducing worry of wine evaporation through barrel pores. Caves have been used to store bottled wine as well,

since the continuing fermentation in the bottle is deterred with cool storage.

For walking through the damp, labyrinthine caves, consider wearing rubber-soled shoes. With such a high humidity level, the cement floors, which are continuously hosed for sanitary purposes, tend to hold small pools of water, so sandals or high heels are bound to be uncomfortable. (A note on high heels in general for touring wineries: leave them in your car. They'll only slow you on gravel, in the fields, and in caves such as these.)

Rutherford Hill Winery grew from the successes of Freemark Abbey. In 1976, Freemark Abbey co-owners Chuck Carpy, Bill Jaeger, and Laurie Wood decided to expand their operation by purchasing the former Souverain of Rutherford winery, which had been built in the early seventies by Joseph Phelps. Later owners were the Pillsbury Mills company and the Bill Jaeger family. Then in 1996, wine importer Anthony Terlato, with sons Bill and John, purchased the winery; they continue to focus its efforts into producing quality Merlot. This medium-sized winery now produces 100,000 cases a year.

Driving to the winery, you'll journey up the hill that also leads to Auberge du Soleil, an elegant resort built Riviera-style along the hill's face. Both the resort and this winery at the crest overlook a picturesque view of the land grant given by pioneer George Yount to his granddaughter in the mid-1800s on the occasion of her marriage to Thomas Rutherford.

The forty-minute tour often opens with an invitation to picnic under the shady oaks bordering a hundred-year-old olive grove. A friendly, open spirit is maintained throughout the tour as you walk from the massive, barn-style hospitality center and winery up a slight incline, to view the spectacular panorama, and then into the cave system. Barrels are stacked four barrels per pallet.

"Each barrel holds about sixty gallons of wine," notes the tour guide. "That's twenty-four cases per barrel." You can almost hear mental calculators whirring as tourists walk past cave after cave of neatly arranged French barrels. Interestingly, the barrels at Rutherford Hill arrive as precut staves, which are then assembled in Napa Valley by coopers at Demptos Cooperage. "We find it advantageous to construct and repair the barrels in our own backyard," the guide explains. The caves hold 8,000 barrels.

After touring a number of wineries, it becomes commonplace to see bungs of varying construction. A bung is the closure for a wine barrel, and some are made of wood, some of plastic or silicone, some of glass, and yet others of earthenware. At Rutherford Hill, questions are frequently raised about paper cups used in place of more solid bungs, with the answer that those barrels are empty for the moment, awaiting washing or new wine.

If you are lucky enough to be led by a tour guide with a resonant voice, be prepared for a pleasant earful as the sound reverberates.

From the caves, the tour moves through the area of ninety stainless steel tanks, their dimpled encasements gleaming in the light. You will learn about various styles of filtration to clarify the wine for eventual bottling, including a state-of-the-art rotary fermenter.

Back at the visitors' center, you will be offered tastes of three wines. (This is one of the few wineries that makes a point of offering free mineral water for designated drivers.) And if you are bound to shop, the retail room at Rutherford Hill offers items from wine chillers to crystal stemware to wine and food books to extra-virgin olive oil and balsamic vinegar.

Whether the fascination is with caves, wine making, or picnicking, Rutherford Hill can provide multiple diversions.

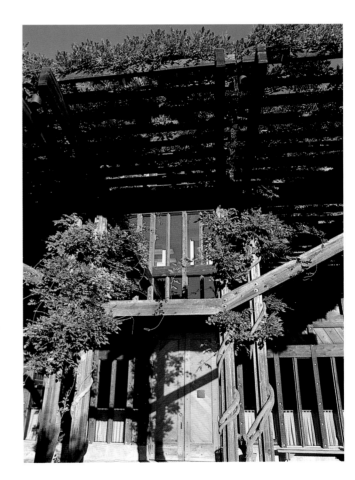

ST. CLEMENT VINEYARDS

St. Clement Vineyards

2867 St. Helena Highway North
St. Helena, CA 94574
(707) 967-3033 and 963-7221
fax (707) 963-1412
Website: www.stclement.com
Email: info@stclement.com

Winemaker: Bill Ballentine
Winery owner: Beringer Wine Estates

Access

Location: Just north of Deer Park Road on the southwest side of Highway 29.

Hours open for visits and tastings: Winter 10 A.M.–4 P.M., summer 10 A.M.–5 P.M., except Easter, Thanksgiving, Christmas, and New Year's Day.

Appointment necessary for tour? Yes, for winery tours, with 1 to 2 hours notice.

Wheelchairs accommodated? Yes.

Tastings

Charge for tasting with tour? No.

Charge for tasting without tour? $2, deductible from price of purchased wine.

Typical wines offered: All current releases of Sauvignon Blanc, Chardonnay, Merlot, Cabernet Sauvignon; often "library wines" as well.

Sales of wine-related items? Yes, including logo glasses ($5) and shirts.

Picnics and Programs

Picnic area open to the public? Yes, by appointment only.

Special events or wine-related programs? "Friends of St. Clement" are sent a newsletter with news of pre-releases and invited to attend the annual Christmas Harvest Festival and Christmas Open Houses.

Immediately following harvest, leaves on the Chinese pistachio trees splash a vibrant red-orange circle of color along the south side of St. Clement Vineyards. This brilliant color contrasts dramatically with subtle gray-green wood siding and white trim on the Victorian home that crowns this western hillside vineyard just up the road from the Charles Krug Winery. Actually, the color of flames is symbolic of the phoenix-like existence this small gem of a winery has known since it was first built in 1876.

Fritz Rosenbaum, a San Francisco glass merchant who wished to join the estate vineyard boom in the Napa Valley, bought this property and constructed the tasteful home atop a small stone winery. The cellar was bonded in 1879, the eighth in the valley. Rosenbaum took great pride in producing his own wine, which he bottled under the name of Johanaberg Vineyards.

During and after Prohibition the winery fell into disrepair, until Michael Robbins, a real estate executive and wine connoisseur, bought the land in 1962 and renamed it Spring

Mountain Vineyards. Robbins took meticulous care in renovating the house, where he lived until he sold it to Dr. William Casey in 1975. At that point, Robbins moved to Tiburcio Parrot's Miravalle estate on Spring Mountain Road, taking with him the Spring Mountain Vineyards name and label.

Once again the elegant little Victorian on the hill took on a new name. Casey named it St. Clement Vineyards, after the small Chesapeake Bay home island of his Maryland family and also in honor of the patron saint of mariners.

Winemaker Chuck Ortman, who had made wines in the same cellars for Mike Robbins' Spring Mountain wines, created the early vintages of Sauvignon Blanc, Chardonnay, and Cabernet Sauvignon under the new label. Dennis Johns, formerly at Sterling Winery, was St. Clement's winemaker for twenty years, and the position is now held by Bill Ballentine. He oversees an annual production of 20,000 cases of wine, making this one of the smaller wineries in the valley.

Sapporo USA, a Japanese brewing and wine-making company seeking to diversify its interests, next purchased Fritz Rosenbaum's Victorian home and cellar in 1987. Under the new proprietors, the winery home finally opened its doors to the public, with daily tastings and tours. This was the first Japanese group to invest in a Napa Valley winery, the number of which has now increased to four. In its most recent metamorphosis, the winery was purchased by Beringer Wine Estates in 1999, with the plan to leave the winery basically untouched.

Climb up the hill from the lower parking area, passing neatly manicured vineyards. The walk is steep, so enjoy the view as you go slowly. You'll stroll past an inviting porch swing and enter the living room–hospitality center where a tasting bar is arranged in a corner of the former dining room. The brief but informative tour departs from the tasting area, passes through the rooms on the first floor, and then moves on to the upper patio just beyond the front door. From there, you'll enjoy a splendid view across and down the valley no matter the season in which you're visiting.

The tour continues under the house in the barrel-lined stone cellar. The scent of fermenting grapes may hit you here more than in larger wineries because of the relatively small dimensions of this space. Wine having been aged in the cellar since the 1880s, that aroma has permeated even the stone and timbers supporting the house.

Out into the daylight and up a gentle hill, you'll come to a newer stone building that houses the fermenting tanks. Most probably you will meet the winemaker, who is open to answering queries about techniques, cold stabilization, the harvest, or whatever is on your mind. The tour guides are extremely friendly, acting more like aunts welcoming visiting relatives than group leaders. The group numbers here tend to mirror the winery's small size—you will probably share the visit with six or fewer travelers. After visiting the fermentation area, a return to the tasting room completes the walking tour and a generous tasting ensues.

There is little wonder why St. Clement's charm has captured many TV commercial producers and is frequently mistaken for a bed and breakfast inn. It stands solitary on its hill, a reminder of the gracious way of life here a century ago.

St. Supéry Vineyards and Winery

8440 St. Helena Highway
Rutherford, CA 94573
(707) 963-4507
fax (707) 963-4526
Website: www.stsupery.com
Email: divinecab@stsupery.com

Winemaker: Michael Scholz
Winery owner: Skalli Corporation

Access

Location: On Highway 29 midway between the towns of Oakville and Rutherford, on the east side of the highway.

Hours open for visits and tastings: June through October 9:30 A.M.–6 P.M., November through May 9:30 A.M.–4:30 P.M., except major holidays.

Appointment necessary for tour? No.

Wheelchairs accommodated? Yes.

Tastings

Charge for tasting with tour? $3, not deductible from price of purchased wine.

Charge for tasting without tour? As above.

Typical wines offered: All current releases of Sauvignon Blanc, Chardonnay, Merlot, Cabernet Sauvignon, and Moscato. Tastings of special collections and library wines for a fee in the Divine Wine Room.

Sales of wine-related items? Yes, including logo glasses ($6.95).

Picnics and Programs

Picnic area open to the public? Yes.

Special events or wine-related programs? Art shows and chamber music concerts.

Wedding gifts at the turn of the last century were occasionally offered in land, rather than lace tablecloths or family photos in silver frames. In fact, this fifty-six-acre winery in the midst of George C. Yount's original five-hundred-acre Rancho Caymus land grant was the dowry gift for Bartlett Vine's marriage to Ellen Yount. She was a daughter of George C. Yount, the prominent landowner who first planted grapestock in the Napa Valley. Later, in 1881, brothers Joseph and Louis Atkinson bought the land and built a home near the hundred-year-old oak tree that shaded a corner of the vineyard. When French winemaker Edward St. Supéry lived in the house, from 1904 to 1920, his home was a magnet for winemakers of the day—Charles Krug, Jacob Beringer, and Jacob Schram were frequent visitors.

A strong sense of history accompanies a visit to St. Supéry, despite the fact that the winery is one of the more recently established estates along Highway 29. Perhaps it is the juxtaposition of the new and the old: the state-of-the-art straight lines of the wine production area contrast with the lush lawn and floral landscaping fronting the Queen Anne Victorian Atkinson house. Or perhaps it is the gracious, old-fashioned hospitality with which tourists are greeted. Among its several lures, the St. Supéry Winery has appeal for all ages and wine appreciation levels.

St. Supéry offers guided as well as unescorted tours. Especially if you arrive during harvest, don't miss the guided tour. It winds from the lobby of the modern winery out through the Atkinson house (which is open for tours only and is decorated with authentic 1880s furnishings appropriate for a summer home) and, past a gazebo, into the exhibition vineyard. There, visitors are encouraged to pick varieties of grapes grown for St. Supéry wines. Of all the winery tours in this collection, only this winery offers you the chance to pick as many grapes as you wish—the closest approximation to "working the crush," which is an unspoken but frequent dream of visitors to the Napa Valley.

While in the vineyard, the tour guide discusses the Dollarhide Ranch, the winery's vineyard of fifteen hundred acres in Pope Valley, northeast of St. Helena. The size alone puts St. Supéry among the largest vineyards for land holdings.

From the vineyard, the tour returns to the production side of the operation. With a 536,000-gallon tank capacity and the ability to bottle 2,500 cases per day, it is no wonder St. Supéry can produce 160,000 cases of its own wines as well as custom crush and bottle for other wineries—working to capacity, you could say.

As the tour continues on a wide catwalk over massive stainless steel tanks, the well-trained guide points out icy buildup on some of the tank walls, due to cold stabilization of white and red wines. When the temperature is dropped well below normal, any sediment in the wine will drop to the bottom of the tank and be easily removed, eliminating visible tartrates. Another plus of a harvest tour here is the outdoor viewing platform directly above the hopper where grapes are received and sent to the crusher-stemmer.

Locals call the St. Supéry self-guided tour "touchy-feely," although the clearly defined walk in the air-conditioned, carpeted space is primarily geared to the senses of sight and smell.

All who previously thought that growing wine grapes was a simple pastime will quickly reconsider when they see a wooden model of a vineyard that is surrounded on four sides with descriptions of the operations of a vineyard year. (See page 21.)

"SmellaVision" is a favorite learning device on the walk-around tour. Here, tourists can smell aromatic essences to help identify the same elements in wine. Using a special display, guests smell cedar, bell pepper, cherry, and black pepper aromas related to red wine aromas. White wine "whiffs" are grapefruit, green olive, dried wildflower, and new-mown hay.

Moving from aromas to wine tasting is a natural step, one that is rewarded with samples of at least five wines. The well-appointed shop offers wines, T-shirts, books on the region, and items related to wine and food.

Culture is very important to the directors of St. Supéry. Be sure to view the changing art shows on display in the entry and tasting areas. And, if you are in the valley for a few days, ask whether the winery is presenting any cultural event, such as a chamber music concert.

SCHRAMSBERG VINEYARDS

Schramsberg
Vineyards

1400 Schramsberg Road
Calistoga, CA 94515
(707) 942-4558
fax (707) 942-2414
Website: www.schramsberg.com
Email: schramsbrg@aol.com

Winemaker: Mike Reynolds
Winery owner: Jamie Davies

Access
Location: 5 miles north of
St. Helena on Highway 29,
turn west onto Peterson
and make a quick right onto
Schramsberg Road.

Hours open for visits and tastings:
By appointments only, Monday–
Saturday, 10 A.M., 11:30 A.M.,
1 P.M., 2:30 P.M. (subject to
change). No tours Thanksgiving and
Christmas.

Appointment necessary for tour?
At least 3 to 5 days before, longer
for weekends.

Wheelchairs accommodated? Yes.

Tastings
Charge for tasting with tour?
$7.50 for three half glasses, not
deductible from cost of purchased
wine. Also, for full pour of library
or tête de cuvée, a separate fee
ranges from $10 to $15.

Charge for tasting without tour?
Tastings offered with tour only.

Typical wines offered: Blanc de
Blancs, Blanc de Noirs, Brut Rosé,
Crémant, Reserve, and J. Schram.

Sales of wine-related items? Yes.

Picnics and Programs
Picnic area open to the public? No.

Special events or wine-related
programs? Yes, Wine Club (call for
details).

The Schramsberg hillside winery and caves epitomize the romance of wine making in the Napa Valley. Very little has changed on the exterior of this estate since it was founded in 1862 by Jacob and Annie Schram, emigrés from Germany. In fact, Jamie Davies and her late husband, Jack, enhanced the property with Victorian gardens and expanded the underground tunnel system to two miles of storage for the sparkling wines made here.

Thousands of visitors travel here every year to encounter the source of Schramsberg's celebrated Napa Valley *méthode champenoise* (aged in the bottle) sparkling wines. The tourists come with the same interest in wine and lifestyle that beckoned Jack and Jamie Davies to the wine country, when they left the Southern California corporate life.

"We call it Napa Valley Champagne," explains Jamie Davies, "because French Champagne is perceived as the finest of that country's sparkling wine. We didn't want to hint at lesser quality here."

Jamie lives in Jacob Schram's original Victorian home with a wide veranda overlooking cascading flowers and the entry to the caves. The home was built in the 1880s, coinciding with winery construction at Beringer, Chateau Montelena, Inglenook, and estates now known as St. Clement and Spring Mountain.

From the 1860s through the turn of the last century, wineries flourished in the Napa Valley, with more than eighteen thousand acres planted to vines by 1900. It was during that early heyday of the local wine industry that Robert Louis Stevenson frequently visited Jacob Schram. Later he devoted a chapter to the Schramsberg estate in his *Silverado Squatters*. (For further information on the famous writer, visit the Robert Louis Stevenson Museum in the town of St. Helena.)

During Prohibition and with a variety of owners, the winery rested. Its hand-dug underground cellar system remained in disrepair until 1965, when the Davies couple came across the Schram Estate after an extensive search for a winery property. They purchased the neglected estate and set about planting Chardonnay, Pinot Noir, and Pinot Blanc vines.

The tour begins at the upper crush-pad area near the parking lot, below the private home. You will pass fragrant plantings of rosemary and other herbs, as well as mulberry trees and palm trees. Most Napa Valley palm trees were planted at the turn of the last century; they were considered exotic status symbols. As you drive the valley's length, note the placement of palms like tufted elephants' legs in the bright Napa sun. Many have been growing a century or more.

Below the house, an amusing bronze statue of a rakish frog, Champagne flute in hand, seems to rise out of the lotus pond fronting the entrance to the caves. Once inside the visitors' center, you'll see numerous photos of VIPs in the worlds of politics, art, and music, all related to menus of dinners where Schramsberg has been served since its first Blanc de Blancs release in 1969.

The cellars are well lit, with rows of poker-table green light fixtures illuminating the walls of Champagne bottles. At least 2 million bottles rest on their sides, with a hundred pounds of pressure in each bottle. The bottles remain dormant until the winemaker decides the proper time for riddling, the turning action that moves the dead yeasts down to the neck of each bottle.

"We house up to six years of vintages of the reserves here," points out the tour guide, "and that's only one of our five styles of Napa Valley Champagne."

Of all the caves in this valley, those at Schramsberg come closest to the ambiance of the catacombs of Paris and other such dank, romantic subterranean cellars. Moss clings to the walls and water oozes from the rocky mountainside.

If you're seeking a hands-on experience, do try the riddling exercise in the caves. Watching master riddler Ramon Viera give rows of Champagne bottles a one-sixth turn makes the symmetrical action seem effortless—until you try it. "Fingers only! Don't use your wrist!" cheerleads the tour guide as visitors volunteer to try their hand—rather, their fingers—at the art. And Ramon's twenty years of riddling forty thousand to sixty thousand bottles daily suddenly make him a hero.

"What happens if a bottle drops?" asks a tourist. He learns that Champagne bottles are much heavier than standard wine bottles to counteract the fermenting pressure; however, a Champagne bottle would shatter into thousands of shards if dropped on cement.

Exiting the cave feels like departing the Tunnel of Love. From corridors of darkness into daylight, you walk to the mechanized arena of wine making: riddling machines there turn five hundred bottles of Blanc de Blancs, reducing the manual work time for those bottles by half. (The other four styles of Schramsberg Champagne are hand riddled.)

Even while you stay behind the yellow line, you will be quite close to the disgorging, corking, and labeling lines in the final stage of this tour. Thirty percent of the pressure and 10 percent of the wine is lost with the disgorging action. You'll hear a dull "thunk, thunk, thunk" as the bottles' metal caps are removed and the frozen plug of sediment flies out of the bottle. Then a small *dosage* of sugar and brandy or cognac or wine is added to sweeten the sparkling wine, followed by immediate corking and labeling.

After seeing the various stages a bottle must endure in this process of making sparkling wine, one tourist remarked that she would never again complain about the cost of a bottle of Napa Valley Champagne.

STAG'S LEAP WINE CELLARS

Stag's Leap Wine Cellars

5766 Silverado Trail
Napa, CA 94558
(707) 944-2020
fax (707) 257-7501
Websites: www.cask23.com
www.stagsleapwinecellars.com
Email: slwc@cask23.com

Winemaker: Michael Silacci
Winery owners:
Warren and Barbara Winiarski

Access
Location: From Napa, take Trancas Street to the Silverado Trail; the winery is 7 miles north on the east side.

Hours open for visits and tastings: 10 A.M.–4:30 P.M. daily, except Easter, Thanksgiving, Christmas, and New Year's Day.

Appointment necessary for tour? Yes.

Wheelchairs accommodated? Yes.

Tastings
Charge for tasting with tour? $2, including logo glass; not deductible from cost of purchased wine.

Charge for tasting without tour? $5.

Typical wines offered: Current releases of Cabernet Sauvignon, Chardonnay, Merlot, Petite Sirah, Sauvignon Blanc, and White Riesling. $5 additional charge for tasting estate wines.

Sales of wine-related items? Yes.

Picnics and Programs
Picnic area open to the public? Yes. Request permission from staff.

Special events or wine-related programs? The *Stag's Leap Wine Cellars News* notifies those on the mailing list of winery activities and special events.

There is a sense of serious dedication to integrity and fine wine making imparted during a visit to Warren and Barbara Winiarski's Stag's Leap Wine Cellars. Since 1970, Warren Winiarski, a former University of Chicago political science lecturer, has insisted on stressing his vines and tightening the space between rows of Cabernet Sauvignon vines, so the roots will stretch as deep as thirty feet in soil he rarely irrigates. This soil lies on the south end of the Stags Leap District, which runs along the Silverado Trail from Clos du Val (just south of Stag's Leap Wine Cellars) to the Oakville Crossroad. To the workers at the winery as well as the Winiarskis, that soil and the grapes harvested annually from the vines are the source of happiness and success.

It was Stag's Leap Wine Cellars' 1973 Cabernet Sauvignon that took highest honors during the pivotal Paris blind tasting in May 1976, when a Napa Valley Chardonnay (Chateau Montelena) and this Cabernet changed the global sea of opinion and earned waves of adulation for California wine. The truly amazing fact is that Winiarski's grapes had been plucked from three-year-old vines, usually considered too immature to produce complex flavor. "That winning gave us the foothold we have today," mentions tour guide Marilyn Landeros.

As you would expect, a man who takes his wines so seriously mirrors his philosophy in tours at this winery. The basic tour here runs about a half-hour; however, Stag's Leap Wine Cellars draws true wine connoisseurs as visitors and their questions often demand detailed explanation. Count on an hour if you are scheduling the day.

You will walk under ancient oak trees based with profuse plantings of ornamental strawberries and wild roses. In summer, the bouquet from the flowers can be overpowering. You will move past the roof-covered fermentation tanks and on to the original crush pad. Occasionally Barbara Winiarski will greet guests and answer a few questions.

"You know, we never imagined we'd need a second phone, much less a second building," she commented about the physical growth of the winery since its 1971 opening. "That's why the five structures on the property have such basic names: Building 1, Building 2, and so on." There is little room here donated to frivolous extras, but tourists will experience an active small winery with a mom-and-pop feel.

Tour guides are extremely well informed and cover such topics as irrigation systems, acidity, brix levels, the effects of drought, and the mix of clay, volcanic soil, and pebbles that creates ideal soil conditions for growing Cabernet Sauvignon grapes. You will pass through the indoor-outdoor fermentation area and then walk uphill to the French oak barrel aging building.

Workers in knee-high rubber boots continue their winery work, moving hoses, climbing the pyramids of barrels to "top off" any air space, and hosing the cement floors to maintain the impeccable conditions necessary to wine.

Discussion will continue about grape types, malolactic fermentation, growers, and microclimates. For some tourists, this visit will include more than they want to know; for others, this will be winery tour heaven.

The tour concludes at the long wooden table in Building 2 where various vintages are poured, including Hawk Crest, the winery's companion label. The tasting moves in standard pattern: first the white wines, followed by the heavier, more tannic red wines. Mineral water is available for designated drivers. By the time of tasting, the small, disparate group of visitors has had a chance to meet and there is a sense of camaraderie, with an occasional exchange of addresses.

The shady picnic area on the face of the winery property just above the parking area offers tables and chairs in a garden setting. This can be a quiet rest stop for motorists and bicyclists as well—all that is needed is "a loaf of bread and thou." The bottle of wine is readily at hand.

Note: There is some confusion concerning punctuation for clarity in the names Stag's Leap Wine Cellars and Stags' Leap Winery and the appellation Stags Leap District. The Stags Leap District appellation was designated officially in the late eighties and is spelled without an apostrophe. Beringer's Stags' Leap Winery connotes a number of stags, whereas Winiarski's wine refers to a single stag.

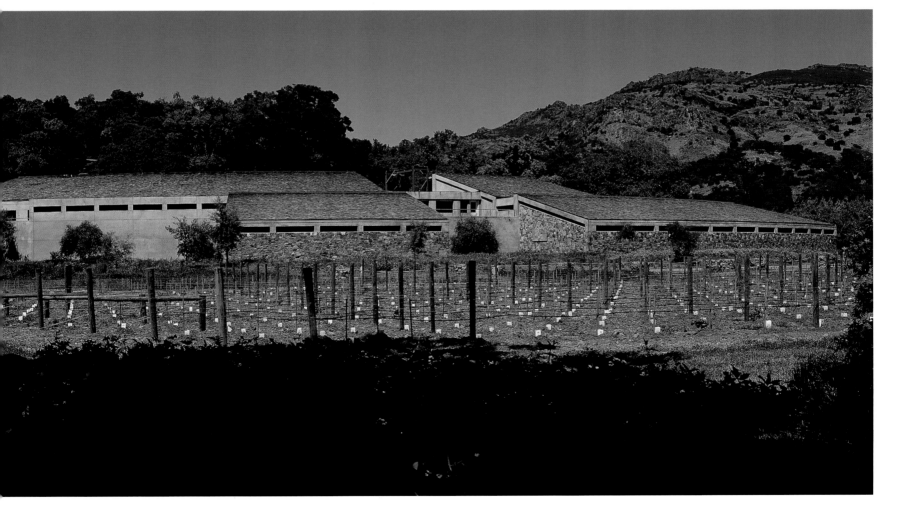

STERLING VINEYARDS

Sterling Vineyards

1111 Dunaweal Lane
Calistoga, CA 94515
(707) 942-3344
fax (707) 942-3467
Website: www.sterlingvineyards.com
Email: See website

Winemaker: Robert Hunter III
Winery owner: Seagram Chateaux
& Estates

Access

Location: 1 mile south of Calistoga
off Dunaweal Lane, between
Highway 29 and the Silverado Trail.

Hours open for visits and tastings:
10:30 A.M.–4:30 P.M. daily,
except Thanksgiving and Christmas.

Appointment necessary for tour? No.

Wheelchairs accommodated? Yes.

Tastings

Charge for tasting with tour? $6,
includes sky tram ride to winery,
tour, self-paced tour, sit-down
tasting of three complimentary
wines, and picnic access.

Charge for tasting without tour?
As above.

Typical wines offered: Current
releases of Chardonnay, Sauvignon
Blanc, Merlot, and Cabernet
Sauvignon.

Sales of wine-related items? Yes.

Picnics and Programs

Picnic area open to the public? Yes.

Special events or wine-related
programs? Special events including
wine and food pairings, barbeques,
wine tasting seminars, and lunches
and dinners. Sterling Wine Club
members are invited to the Bud
Break Festival, Holiday Party, and
Valentine's Dinner. For group
events, contact the Special Events
department.

The panoramic vista from the bell-tower deck at Sterling Vineyards is one of the most spectacular in the Napa Valley. From there you will see mountain ranges encircling the valley floor, with a sweep broad enough to include Highway 29 and the Silverado Trail in one glance. During the spring, rust-colored farmsteads and bright blue reservoirs contrast with a central carpet of yellow mustard flowers blooming at the base of dormant rootstock. And in the Mediterranean style of this winery, olive trees and cypresses frame the extensive property.

When the winery was built, in 1971, the idea was to create a place of prominence by placing its pure white arches, towers, and castle-like walls high above the valley floor. At the same time, architect Martin Waterfield constructed a cool mountainside area for the chai (barrel aging area) by building it vertically into the hill and lighting it through gemlike stained glass windows.

Because of the labyrinthine driving paths and the narrow roads to the top of the estate, a sky tram (six dollars per person) was devised to transport visitors over gardens, vineyards, and a small lake to the arrival dock, where a self-guided tour begins. Follow the informational placards to learn about wine making in the grand style. Sterling, which is owned by the Seagram Chateau & Estates Wine Company, produces eleven varietal wines here from grapes grown on its 1,100 acres of Napa Valley vines, and has a fermentation capacity of almost five hundred thousand gallons. The signs will direct you from station to station and, even on a busy day, you'll rarely have the sense of being in a crowd.

There is quite a bit of walking up and down stairs on this visit, including a steep climb to the final tasting room stop. On a blisteringly hot day, take it slowly.

Once in the tasting room area, you can relax in the spacious air-conditioned interior or you may choose to sit on the outdoor patio. From the terraces, you'll look through pines, redwoods, and some oaks up-valley toward Calistoga. Clos Pegase winery is in view, as are occasional gliders from the Calistoga airport nearby.

While in the visitors' center, you'll learn of The Seagram Classics School of Service and Hospitality, which offers classes primarily for members of the restaurant and wine industry. There is also St. Dunstan's dining room, decorated in medieval style and available for private dinners.

By the time of descent via tram to the parking lot, you will have learned a considerable amount about wine making and you'll have been to the top of the world in the middle of the valley.

SUTTER HOME WINERY

Sutter Home Winery

277 St. Helena Highway
St. Helena, CA 94574
(707) 963-3104
fax (707) 963-9163
Website: www.sutterhome.com
Email: info@sutterhome.com

Winemaker: Liz Oberschulte
Winery owner: The Trinchero family

Access

Location: 1 mile south of St. Helena on the west side of Highway 29, at the large white Victorian.

Hours open for visits and tastings: Retail store open 10 A.M.–5:30 P.M.; Tasting Room open 10 A.M.–5 P.M., except Easter, Thanksgiving, Christmas, and New Year's Day.

Appointment necessary for tour? No. Self-guided garden tours.

Wheelchairs accommodated? In tasting room, not in gardens.

Tastings

Charge for tasting with tour? No.

Charge for tasting without tour? No.

Typical wines offered: Current releases of White Zinfandel, Sauvignon Blanc, Chardonnay, Chenin Blanc, Zinfandel, Reserve Zinfandel, and Cabernet Sauvignon.

Sales of wine-related items? Yes, including four logo glasses (prices vary, $2.95–$5.95).

Picnics and Programs

Picnic area open to the public? No.

Special events or wine-related programs? Blend Your Own Wine Program; call tasting room for details. Special garden tours are offered Wednesday–Sunday, 11 A.M.–3 P.M., on the hour. The *Sutter Home Newsletter* features new releases and recipes.

If an easy self-tour is your goal in visiting a winery, Sutter Home is an ideal destination. The visit to this winery, known largely for its White Zinfandel but home to a wide range of wines, consists of walking around the perimeter of a large room with a central wine-tasting bar. Beyond the tasting, you have the option to actually blend your own wine, a process that is more fun than a chem lab experiment and which yields a personally labeled bottle of wine after the hour to hour-and-a-half experience. Call ahead for this option.

Inside the winery's visitors' center, there is no treatment of vineyards and grapes, with the exception of a display of old wine production machines, some photos of wine-making procedures, and a placard that presents the story of the winery. Wine is described as an enhancement to daily life in the style of the good old days.

But the natural is also celebrated, in the present-day garden just outside the visitors' center, which is alive with eight hundred varieties of flowers, trees, and plants in the beds surrounding the 1884 Victorian home on the property. Garden tours are available and well worth the walk. You'll see beds of exquisite roses, scented geraniums, free-form wisteria, butterfly bushes, and trees such as weeping flowering cherry and Japanese maple. If photographing flowers is a hobby for you, be sure to visit Sutter Home midsummer for the best color and floral varieties.

Although the home is closed to the public, tourists are encouraged to rest in the garden gazebo and relax, remembering a time when life was slower.

The Trinchero family, which now owns Sutter Home, traces the winery's history back to 1890, when it was the first wooden winery in the valley. "The story of Sutter Home is a slice of Americana," reads the notice at the interior entry to the tasting room. "Its fate rose and fell with impacts of World Wars I and II, with Prohibition, the Depression, the Great Immigration of Europeans to the United States and the San Francisco earthquake and fire of 1906. That year, Sutter Home, every acre, every building, was sold for $10 gold." Today's Sutter Home, which rose to success on the wings of White Zinfandel's popularity in the 1970s and 1980s, is one of the most profitable wineries in the country. Its actual (and huge) wine production area is a few miles away, off Zinfandel Lane, where nearly 10 million cases of wine are produced annually from Napa Valley and other California grapes. But the winery center on Highway 29 just south of St. Helena continues to draw thousands of tourists who yearn to trace the roots of their favorite wine—"White Zin."

Trefethen Vineyards

1160 Oak Knoll Avenue
Napa, CA 94588
(707) 255-7700
fax (707) 255-0793
Website: www.trefethen.com
Email: winery@trefethen.com

Winemaker: Peter Luthi
Winery owners:
Janet and John Trefethen

Access

Location: 2 miles north of the town of Napa, take Oak Knoll Avenue to the Trefethen entrance.

Hours open for visits and tastings: 10 A.M.–4:30 P.M. daily, except New Year's Day, Easter, Thanksgiving, and Christmas; tours given at 10:30 A.M. and 2:30 P.M.

Appointment necessary for tour? Yes, 24 hours in advance.

Wheelchairs accommodated? Limited.

Tastings

Charge for tasting with tour? Some complimentary tasting. $5 fee for Reserve and limited release tasting.

Charge for tasting without tour? Yes, $4, includes glass.

Typical wines offered: Current, Reserve and Library Selection releases of Chardonnay and Cabernet Sauvignon as well as dry Riesling, Merlot, and Cabernet.

Sales of wine-related items? Yes, including books, logo glasses, and shirts.

Picnics and Programs

Picnic area open to the public? No.

Special events or wine-related programs? Napa Valley Cooking Class, Trefethen Connection Wine Club.

The Trefethen family has a deep pride in its six hundred contiguous acres of vineyards, one of the largest plots under single ownership within Napa Valley. As a result, tourists quickly learn the history of the land and how it relates to the winery estate.

The drive onto the property from Oak Knoll Avenue can be reached easily from the Silverado Trail or Highway 29. As you enter, signs mark clearly the various grape varieties—Pinot Noir, Chardonnay, Cabernet Sauvignon. The old winery dominates the property with its massive form, painted the Tuscan orange of a winter sunset.

Founded in 1886, the former Eshcol winery was the earliest three-story gravity-flow winery in the county. It produced wine until 1940, with a hiatus during Prohibition (1919–1933), during which time the government granted permission for making sacramental or personal-use wines only.

Vestiges of earlier days are evident in the visitors' entry room where the tour begins. You'll see photos of the land when it was planted to walnut and prune orchards and as it was in 1968, when Gene and Katie Trefethen chose this 600-acre parcel of land with the dream of remodeling the Eshcol winery and planting grapes once again. "We are a destination winery," declares a guide to a small group of tourists. "Fifty percent of our visitors already know Trefethen wines and are willing to drive here to find us," he adds, "and we prefer people who are interested in wine." There is the advantage in an intimate-size group that you can stop at any point and ask questions, which are encouraged and are answered in depth.

This is a "backwards" tour, in the sense that the first areas you'll visit—the barrel aging rooms—are not first in the sequence of wine making. But since Trefethen was a gravity-flow winery originally, it makes sense to see barrels where they used to rest over a hundred years ago.

In a gravity-flow winery, grapes are crushed, stemmed, and fermented on the top floor. The fermented juice is next aged in barrels on the second floor, then rolled to the ground level for bottling and shipping.

The stairs to the second floor of the winery are narrow. You'll view a majority of small oak barrels, which hold enough wine to fill 325,000 750-milliliter bottles. Note the silicone bungs in the barrels. These barrel stoppers are made of

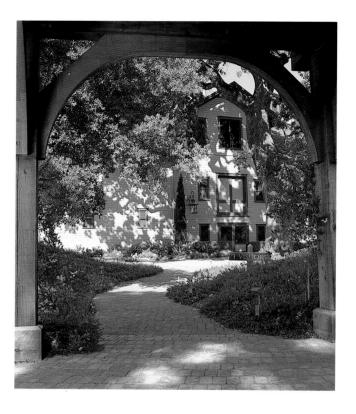

an inert material that provides a tighter seal than the standard wooden bungs.

Wherever you tour Napa Valley wineries, you will hear discussion of the "toast" of the oak in various wines. Trefethen Vineyards makes the effort to discriminate the various stages of toastiness: there is a display of woods from six different oak barrel interiors, each of which has been carefully charred to develop a certain level of toasted oak flavor. Later, during wine tasting, the tour guide will point out the "toast" quality of the various wines.

Moving from the main building, the tour passes the crush pad and crusher-stemmer. During harvest, you are in clear view of grape delivery and all the swift stages that take place from arrival of the hand-picked grapes in open-topped gondolas (fruit-bearing trailers) to the fermentation stage. The fermentation tanks, bottling line, and other stages of production are quite accessible. "Everything you see," points out the guide, "from vine to bottle, is done on our land. Therefore, it can be called 'estate bottled'—all our wines are estate bottled."

V. SATTUI WINERY

V. Sattui Winery

1111 White Lane
St. Helena, CA 94574
(707) 963-7774
telefax (707) 963-4324
Website: www.vsattui.com
Email: info@vsattui.com

Winemaker: Rick Rosenbrand
Winery owner: Darryl Sattui

Access

Location: On Highway 29, ½ mile
south of St. Helena, right across
from the Beacon service station.

Hours open for visits and tastings:
9 A.M.–6 P.M. daily, March through
October; 9 A.M.–5 P.M., November
through February, except Christmas
Day.

Appointment necessary for tour?
Not for self-guided tours; private
tours and groups do require
appointments.

Wheelchairs accommodated? Yes.

Tastings

Charge for tasting with tour? Not
with self-guided tour; private/
group tour and tasting charge is
$75 per group or $2.50 per person,
whichever is greater. Not deductible
from price of purchased wine.

Charge for tasting without tour? No.

Typical wines offered: Current
releases of at least eight wines,
featuring Sauvignon Blanc,
Chardonnay, and Johannisberg
Riesling. Also, estate Gamay Rouge,
Zinfandel, and Cabernet Sauvignon.

Sales of wine-related items?
Yes, including logo glasses.

Picnics and Programs

Picnic area open to the public? Yes.
Special events or wine-related
programs? The Wine of the Month
program; Cellar Club private tasting
for members.

Cheese and picnics, picnics and cheese. Napa Valley tourists' first impressions of the V. Sattui Winery just south of St. Helena relate to picnics, due to the two acres of shaded tables and benches fronting Highway 29. Beds of flowers, ancient oak trees, and a wine tasting room and delicatessen enhance the visual invitation to turn off the road and relax.

Since the Napa Valley weather is relatively clement, about 300,000 visitors take advantage of the picnic area year-round. An Italian-style stone building dominates the land, with multilevel terraces, porches, and fountains decorating the front of the building.

This winery (built in 1975, although it appears older) is a far cry from Vittorio Sattui's Bryant Avenue Winery in San Francisco's North Beach. That company produced wine from 1885 to 1921 and then closed due to Prohibition. It was not until Vittorio's great-grandson, Daryl Sattui, reestablished the winery and moved it to St. Helena that the family name was again affiliated with wine.

The tour at V. Sattui is an extremely relaxed self-tour. As you walk the property and visit the various levels of the winery, you'll find signs describing the history of the ancient artifacts arranged outdoors, such as antique carts that used to transport wine in barrels. You are free to roam, to picnic, and to shop in the large retail store that offers breads, cheeses, wine, deli-style foods, and wine-related items. In fact, V. Sattui is one of the largest distributors of imported cheese in Northern California.

Despite the picnic atmosphere, the emphasis is on making wine of fine quality. There is a barrel-lined underground stone wine cellar where weddings, private tastings, and meetings take place. The winery produces 30,000 cases annually and keeps its overhead low by selling all its wine through the tasting room, along with cheese and picnics, picnics and cheese.

RESOURCES

Note: All resources are in the 707 Telephone Area Code

CHAMBERS OF COMMERCE

CALISTOGA CHAMBER OF COMMERCE
1458 Lincoln Avenue, Calistoga
942-6333

NAPA CHAMBER OF COMMERCE
1556 First Street, Napa
226-7455

ST. HELENA CHAMBER OF COMMERCE
1020 Main Street, St. Helena
963-4456

YOUNTVILLE CHAMBER OF COMMERCE
6516 Yount Street, Yountville
944-0904

EDUCATIONAL SOURCES

BERINGER'S CULINARY ARTS CENTER
Beringer Vineyards
2000 Main Street, St. Helena
963-7115

THE CULINARY INSTITUTE OF AMERICA
Greystone Cellars
2555 Main Street, St. Helena
967-1100

MEADOWOOD WINE SCHOOL
Meadowood Resort
900 Meadowood Lane,
St. Helena
963-3636

NAPA VALLEY COLLEGE
2277 Napa-Vallejo Highway,
Napa
255-3000

SEAGRAM CLASSICS SCHOOL OF SERVICE AND HOSPITALITY
Post Office Box 365, Calistoga
942-0852

LIBRARIES

CALISTOGA LIBRARY
1108 Myrtle Street, Calistoga
942-4833

NAPA COUNTY LIBRARY
580 Coombs Street, Napa
255-4241 or 800-248-8402

NAPA VALLEY WINE LIBRARY
1492 Library Lane, St. Helena
(within St. Helena Library)
963-5145

ST. HELENA LIBRARY
1492 Library Lane, St. Helena
963-5244

YOUNTVILLE LIBRARY
6548 Yount Street, Yountville
944-1888

MUSEUMS

BALE GRIST MILL
California State Park System
On Highway 29 between
St. Helena and Calistoga, on the
west side of the road
962-2236

CALISTOGA CITY MUSEUM
1511 Washington Street,
Calistoga
942-5911

THE DIROSA PRESERVE
5200 Carneros Highway, Napa
226-5991

THE HESS COLLECTION
4411 Redwood Road, Napa
255-1144

NAPA VALLEY MUSEUM
55 Presidents Circle, Yountville
944-0500

ROBERT LOUIS STEVENSON MUSEUM
Silverado Museum
1490 Library Lane, St. Helena
963-3757

SHARPSTEEN MUSEUM
1511 Washington Street,
Calistoga
942-5911

NEWSPAPERS

THE WEEKLY CALISTOGAN
1328 Main Street, St. Helena
942-6242

NAPA REGISTER
1615 Second Street, Napa
226-3711

ST. HELENA STAR
1328 Main Street, St. Helena
963-2731

MAGAZINES

APPELLATION
1700 Soscol, Suite 2, Napa
255-2525

ON TOURING WINERIES

Touring most Napa Valley wineries is gratis or with a nominal charge for the wines tasted or for a wine glass bearing a winery's logo.

Like restaurants, many wineries prefer to know their guest count, for obvious reasons. Although phone numbers are rarely taken when you book a tour, it is polite to call in to cancel. A tour guide may be brought in just for your party, particularly at the smaller wineries.

It is ideal to arrive at least five minutes before a tour, leaving time to locate and join the tour group.

In most cases, it is acceptable to arrive just before a tour and join in, but at wineries that request reservations, politeness suggests calling ahead, even that same morning.

Stay with the group, remembering that these are working wineries.

Expect noise from tractors, bottling machines, forklifts and other equipment. In other words, be prepared for action.

On attire: casual clothing is the norm. After all, you'll be visiting working areas that often include newly turned earth or moist floors. Even on a blisteringly hot day, you may wish to bring a light wrap for touring the caves and wineries. They are air-conditioned to around fifty-five degrees, whether by nature or by machines, and the contrast in temperature is noticeable.

On footwear: it's a good idea to wear rubber-soled shoes. Since the winery business must be as sanitary as the dairy business, cleanliness is very important. Therefore, the floors of the winery are frequently wet from hosings. Also, closed-toe shoes are recommended for visiting wineries that include vineyard tours.

Some people collect etched wine glasses from the various wineries that sell such stemware.

Small wineries are willing to talk of distributors in specific areas; large wineries don't need to. But if you wish to know how to find a certain wine in your hometown, do not hesitate to ask the tour guide.

It's not necessary to drink all the wine offered during a tasting. Use the dump buckets or spit buckets that are placed on the tasting bars for that purpose.

During any tour, expect a variety of levels of wine knowledgeability among the visitors. Don't be shy about asking questions.

Tour guides are often excellent sources for restaurant recommendations.

It is illegal to serve wine to minors, which includes anyone under the age of twenty-one.

There is no smoking in cellars or tasting rooms.

You are encouraged to take photographs.

ON WINE AND WINE MAKING

Wine is fermented grape juice.

There is only one harvest annually, in the autumn.

The local name for the harvest is "the crush."

The vintage year on a bottle refers to the year the grapes were picked.

Wine derives its natural sugar from the fruit itself; it is illegal to add sugar to wines in California.

Grapes do not like "wet feet." There is little irrigation in the miles of vineyards. The grape rootstock has long roots, which seek the natural water level as deep as thirty feet underground.

Every state in the nation, except Alaska, grows grapes to make wine.

California grows more than 75 percent of the country's wine grapes, 90 percent of the table grapes, and all the raisin grapes.

The Napa Valley holds approximately 31,000 acres of land planted to vineyards, which yields only 4 percent of the state's wine grapes.

To store wine while driving in the valley, keep it upright within the car (presuming you have not opened the bottle). The temperature inside a closed automobile can easily reach 110 degrees. Do not store wine in the trunk, particularly during extreme heat; the trunk will act as an oven and actually cook the wine.

A telltale sign that the wine has been overheated is a leaking bottle. This is caused by the contraction and expansion of the cork in response to the drastic change in temperature.

One plastic lug full of grapes holds forty pounds of fruit.

Sparkling wine is popularly served in stemware called a flute. The flat coupe-shaped Champagne glasses popular in the past were said to have been based on the form of Marie Antoinette's left breast.

Notice the shapes of still wine bottles. Those with "sloping shoulders" are based on techniques used originally in the Burgundy region of France. Those with "square shoulders" are based on wines of the Bordeaux region. Historically, the reason for shouldering wine bottles was for tax purposes: the tax collector could define the source of the wine by "reading the shoulders."

Wine is the only alcoholic beverage that improves with aging after bottling and corking.

September first is often the date for prices for newly released wines.

Check with your tour guide about shipping wine home. In most cases, it is illegal to ship from the winery and there are limits to mailing wine to certain states at this time. There are local wine shops and shipping companies which can handle the transport process for you if you live in a state which allows shipping.

These are the graduated sizes of wine bottles:

Half Bottle (Tenth).. 375 milliliters
Standard Bottle..750 milliliters
Magnum..................................2 standard bottles, 1.5 liters
Double Magnum.......................4 standard bottles, 3 liters
Jeroboam.................................6 standard bottles, 4.5 liters
Rehoboam.........................6 bottles Champagne, 4.5 liters
Methuselah...........................8 bottles Champagne, 6 liters
Imperial......................................8 standard bottles, 6 liters
Salmanazar..............................12 standard bottles, 9 liters
Balthazar..................................16 standard bottles, 12 liters
Nebuchadnezzar....................20 standard bottles, 15 liters

ON BARRELS

Wine aging barrels, cut in half, are often available, for example for use as planters or table bases. Ask your tour guide whether the winery has any for sale or where they can be found nearby.

A "barrel tasting" refers to tasting wine directly out of the aging barrel before the wine has been bottled. (It has nothing to do with tasting the barrel itself!)

A full barrel contains 498 pounds of wine. Including the fifty-pound barrel, the weight is near 550 pounds.

New French barrels cost around $700.

New American barrels cost around $350.

One French barrel holds sixty gallons, the equivalent of twenty-five cases of wine.

Each case of wine holds nine liters of beverage.

American oak barrels are made in Tennessee, Kentucky, Ohio, and California.

French barrels have full, broad "bellies" with wide space between steel bands at the center; American barrels are more uniformly shaped, with steel bands at relatively even widths across the barrel.

Barrels are often stacked on wooden triangular wedges. Also, you will see them on wooden pallets, steel squared-off frames, and on wooden frames.

If red-wine barrels seem old and stained compared to pristine white-wine barrels, your observation is correct. Grape juice for red wines is colored by steeping it on the grape skins. The resultant red color stains barrels and gives them an appearance of age.

DIRECTORY

A Directory of Napa Valley Wineries

Note: All wineries are in the 707 Telephone Area Code

ACACIA WINERY
2750 Las Amigas Road
Napa 94559
226-9991

AETNA SPRINGS CELLARS
7227 Pope Valley Road
Pope Valley 94567
965-2675

ALTAMURA WINERY
1700 Silverado Trail
Napa 94558
253-2000

AMIZETTA VINEYARDS
1099 Greenfield Road
St. Helena 94574
963-1053

S. ANDERSON VINEYARDS
1473 Yountville Crossroad
Yountville 94599
944-8642
sawines@4bubbly.com
www.4bubbly.com

ANDERSON'S CONN VALLEY VINEYARDS
680 Rossi Road
St. Helena 94574
963-8600
cvvcab@aol.com

ANDRETTI WINERY
4162 Big Ranch Road
Napa 94558
259-6777
www.andrettiwinery.com

ARNS WINERY
601 Mund Road
St. Helena 94574
963-3429
www.arnswine@napanet.net

ARROYO WINERY
2361 Greenwood Road
Calistoga 94515
942-6995

ARTESA WINERY
1345 Henry Road
Napa 94558
224-9601
www.artesawinery.com

DAVID ARTHUR VINEYARDS
1519 Sage Canyon Road
St. Helena 94574
963-5190
www.DavidArthur.com

ARTISAN WINE COMPANY
1216 Church Street
St. Helena 94574
968-9463

ATLAS PEAK VINEYARDS
3700 Soda Canyon Road
Napa 94558
252-7971
www.AtlasPeak.com

AZALEA SPRINGS
4301 Azalea Springs Way
Calistoga 94515
942-4811

BALLENTINE VINEYARDS
2820 St. Helena
    Highway North
St. Helena 94574
963-7919

BARNETT VINEYARDS
4070 Spring Mountain Road
St. Helena 94574
963-0802
barnett@napanet.net

BEAUCANON
1695 St. Helena Highway
St. Helena 94574
967-3520
Beaucanon_winery@msn.com

BEAULIEU VINEYARDS
1960 St. Helena Highway
Rutherford 94573
967-5200
www.bvwine.com

BENESSERE VINEYARDS
1010 Big Tree Road
St. Helena 94574
963-5853
www.BenessereVineyards.com

BERINGER VINEYARDS
2000 Main Street
St. Helena 94574
963-7115
www.beringer.com

BETTINELLI VINEYARDS
7850 Silverado Trail
Oakville 94952
967-4141
info@bettinelli.com
www.bettinelli.com

BLOCKHEDIA, LORENZA-LAKE WINERY
1764 Scott Street
St. Helena 94574
963-8593

BOUCHAINE VINEYARDS
1075 Buchli Station Road
Napa 94558
252-9065

BUEHLER VINEYARDS
820 Greenfield Road
St. Helena 94574
963-2155
www.BuehlerVineyards.com

BURGESS CELLARS
1108 Deer Park Road
St. Helena 94574
963-4766
www.BurgessCellars.com

CAFARO CELLARS
1591 Dean York Lane
St. Helena 94574
963-7181
jcafaro@pacbell.net

CAIN CELLARS
3800 Langtry Road
St. Helena 94574
963-1616
winery@cainfive.com

CAKEBREAD CELLARS
8300 St. Helena Highway
Rutherford 94573
963-5221
cellars@cakebread.com
www.cakebread.com

CALAFIA CELLARS
629 Fulton Street
St. Helena 94574
963-0114

CARDINALE ESTATE
P.O. Box 328
Oakville 94562
944-2807

CARNEROS CREEK WINERY
1285 Dealy Lane
Napa 94558
253-9563
wineinfo@carneros-creek.com
www.carneros-creek.com

CASA NUESTRA
3451 Silverado Trail
St. Helena 94574
963-5783

CAYMUS VINEYARDS
8700 Conn Creek Road
Rutherford 94573
963-4204

CHAPPELLET VINEYARD
1581 Sage Canyon Road
St. Helena 94574
963-7136
winery@chappellet.com

CHATEAU BOSWELL
3468 Silverado Trail
St. Helena 94574
963-0351

CHATEAU CHEVALIER
3101 Spring Mountain Road
St. Helena 94574
963-2342

CHATEAU CHEVRE WINERY
2030 Hoffman Lane
Yountville 94599
944-2184

CHATEAU MONTELENA
1429 Tubbs Lane
Calistoga 94515
942-5105
www.montelena.com

CHATEAU POTELLE
3875 Mount Veeder Road
Napa 94558
255-9440
info@chateaupotelle.com
www.chateaupotelle.com

CHATEAU WOLTNER
150 White Cottage Road South
Angwin 94508
965-2445

CHIMNEY ROCK WINERY
5350 Silverado Trail
Napa 94558
257-2641
retail@chimneyrock.com
www.chimneyrock.com

CLARK-CLAUDON
    VINEYARDS
P.O. Box 15
St. Helena 94574
965-9393

CLOS DU VAL
5330 Silverado Trail
Napa 94558
259-2225
cdv@closduval.com
www.closduval.com

CLOS PEGASE
1060 Dunaweal Lane
Calistoga 94515
942-4981
cp@clospegase.com
www.clospegase.com

CONN CREEK WINERY
8711 Silverado Trail
St. Helena 94574
963-5133

CORISON WINES
981 St. Helena Highway South
St. Helena 94574
963-0826
www.corison.com

COSENTINO WINERY
7415 St. Helena Highway
Yountville 94599
944-1220
finewines@cosentino.com
www.cosentino.com

COSTELLO VINEYARDS
1200 Orchard Avenue
Napa 94558
252-8483

CRICHTON HALL
    VINEYARD
1150 Darms Lane
Napa 94558
224-4200
chvine@pacbell.net

CUVAISON
4550 Silverado Trail
Calistoga 94515
942-6266
info@cuvaison.com
www.cuvaison.com

DALLA VALLE VINEYARDS
7776 Silverado Trail
Napa 94558
944-2676

DARIOUSH
4240 Silverado Trail
Napa 94558
257-2345
www.darioush.com

DEER PARK WINERY
1000 Deer Park Road
Deer Park 94576
963-5411

DIAMOND CREEK
    VINEYARDS
1500 Diamond Mountain Road
Calistoga 94515
942-6926

DOMAINE CARNEROS
1240 Duhig Road
Napa 94559
257-0101
www.domainecarneros.com

DOMAINE CHANDON
1 California Drive
Yountville 94599
944-2280
dchandon@napanet.net
www.chandon.com

DOMAINE CHARBAY
    WINERY
4001 Spring Mountain Road
St. Helena 94574
963-9327
miles@domainecharbay.com
www.charbay.com

DOMAINE MONTREAUX
4242 Big Ranch Road
Napa 94558
253-2802
wine@montiavovineyards.com

DOMINUS ESTATE
2570 Napanook Road
Yountville 94562
944-8954
dominus@napanet.net
www.dominusestate.com

DUCKHORN VINEYARDS
1000 Lodi Lane
St. Helena 94574
963-7108
info@duckhornvineyards.com
www.duckhorn.com

DUNN VINEYARDS
805 White Cottage Road
Angwin 94508
965-3642

DUTCH HENRY WINERY
4300 Silverado Trail
Calistoga 94515
942-5771
wine@dutchhenry.com
www.dutchhenry.com

EAGLE & ROSE ESTATE
1844 Pope Canyon Road
Pope Valley 94567
965-9463

EDGEWOOD ESTATE
401 St. Helena Highway South
St. Helena 94574
963-2335

EHLERS GROVE/
    CARTLIDGE & BROWNE
    WINERY
3222 Ehlers Lane
St. Helena 94574
963-3200
ehlers@napanet.net
www.ehlersgrove.com

ELKHORN PEAK CELLARS
200 Polson Road
Napa 94558
255-0504
epcellars@aol.com
www.elkhornpeak.com

EL MOLINO
P.O. Box 306
St. Helena 94574
963-3632
elmolino@fcs.net

HANS FAHDEN VINEYARDS
4855 Petrified Forest Road
Calistoga 94515
942-6760
antone@hansfahden.com
www.hansfahden.com

FARELLA-PARK VINEYARDS
2222 Third Avenue
Napa 94558
254-9489

FAR NIENTE WINERY
1 Acacia Drive
Oakville 94562
944-2861
welcome@farniente.com
www.farniente.com

FIFE VINEYARDS
Spring Mountain
St. Helena 94574
963-1534
redhead@fifevineyards.com

FLORA SPRINGS WINERY
677 St. Helena Highway South
    (tasting room)
1978 West Zinfandel Lane
St. Helena 94574
967-8032
www.floraprings.com

FOLIE À DEUX
3070 St. Helena Highway
St. Helena 94574
963-1160
www.flavorweb.com/folie.htm

FORMAN VINEYARDS
1501 Big Rock Road
St. Helena 94574
963-0234

FRANCISCAN OAKVILLE
    ESTATES
1178 Galleron Road
Rutherford 94573
963-7111

FRANUS WINE COMPANY
2055 Hoffman Lane
Napa 94558
945-0542

FREEMARK ABBEY WINERY
3022 St. Helena Highway
St. Helena 94574
963-9694
www.freemarkabbey.com

FRISINGER CELLARS
2277 Dry Creek Road
Napa 94558
255-3749

FROG'S LEAP WINERY
3358 St. Helena Highway
St. Helena 94574
963-4704
ribbit@frogsleap.com
www.frogsleap.com

GIRARD WINERY
500 Oakville Crossroad
Oakville 94562
944-8577

GOOSECROSS CELLARS
1119 State Lane
Yountville 94599
944-1986
dtopper@napanet.net
www.goosecross.com

GRACE FAMILY VINEYARD
1210 Rockland Road
St. Helena 94574
963-0808

GRAESER WINERY
255 Petrified Forest Road
Calistoga 94515
942-4437
www.graeserwinery.com

GREEN AND RED VINEYARD
3208 Chiles Pope Valley Road
St. Helena 94574
965-2346

GRGICH HILLS CELLARS
1829 St. Helena Highway
Rutherford 94573
963-2784

GROTH VINEYARDS
750 Oakville Crossroad
Oakville 94562
944-0290
www.grothwines.com

GUILLAMS VINEYARDS
3851 Spring Mountain Road
St. Helena 94574
963-9059

HAGAFEN CELLARS
P.O. Box 3035
Napa 94558
252-0781
hagafen@aol.com
www.hagafen.com

HARLAN ESTATE
1551 Oakville Grade
Oakville 94562
944-1441

HARRISON VINEYARDS
1527 Sage Canyon Road
St. Helena 94574
963-8726
sofia@interx.net

HAVENS WINE CELLARS
1441 Calistoga Avenue
Napa 94558
255-7337
havenswine@earthlink.net

HEITZ WINE CELLARS
436 St. Helena Highway
St. Helena 94574
963-3542
www.heitzcellar.com

HELENA VIEW/
   JOHNSTONE VINEYARDS
3500 Highway 128
Calistoga 94515
942-4956

THE HESS COLLECTION
   WINERY
4411 Redwood Road
Napa 94558
255-1144
www.hesscollection.com

WILLIAM HILL WINERY
1761 Atlas Peak Road
Napa 94558
224-4477
www.williamhill.com

HONIG CELLARS
850 Rutherford Road
Rutherford 94573
963-5618
www.honigwine.com

JARVIS
2970 Monticello Road
Napa 94558
255-5280
wines@jarvisnapa.com
www.jarvisnapa.com

JESSUP CELLARS
3377 Solano Avenue, Suite 402
Napa 94558
224-7067
wine@jessupcellars.com
www.jessupcellars.com

JUDD'S HILL
P.O. Box 415
St. Helena 94574
963-9093
www.juddshill.com

KATE'S VINEYARD
5211 Big Ranch Road
Napa 94558
255-2644

ROBERT KEENAN WINERY
3660 Spring Mountain Road
St. Helena 94574
963-9177
rhkeenan@community.net

KELHAM-MACLEAN
   WINERY
360 Zinfandel Lane
St. Helena 94574
963-2000

KORNELL CELLARS/
   FRANK ROMBAUER
   CELLARS
1091 Larkmead Lane
St. Helena 94574
942-0859

CHARLES KRUG WINERY
2800 Main Street
St. Helena 94574
963-5057
charleskrug@pmondavi.com

LA FAMIGLIA DI ROBERT
   MONDAVI
1595 Oakville Grade
Oakville 94562
944-2811
www.robertmondavi.com

LAIL VINEYARDS
P.O. Box 249
Rutherford 94573
967-0707
Rlail@mindspring.com

LA JOTA VINEYARD
1102 Las Posadas Road
Angwin 94508
965-2878

LAMBORN FAMILY
   VINEYARDS
2075 Summit Lake Drive
Angwin 94508
967-8231
bobl@napanet.net

LARKMEAD VINEYARDS
P.O. Box 309
St. Helena 94574
942-6605
bakerc@fbm.com

LIMUR WINERY
771 Sage Canyon Road
St. Helena 94574
963-3726
bobl@napanet.net

LIPARITA CELLARS
410 La Fata Street #200
St. Helena 94574
963-2775
julia@liparita.com
www.liparita.com

LIVINGSTON WINES
1895 Cabernet Lane
St. Helena 94574
963-2120
livcab@aol.com

LONG MEADOW RANCH
1775 Whitehall Lane
St. Helena 94574
963-4555
info@longmeadowranch.com
www.longmeadowranch.com

LONG VINEYARDS
1535 Sage Canyon Road
St. Helena 94574
963-2496
info@longvineyards.com
www.longvineyards.com

LUNA VINEYARDS
2921 Silverado Trail
Napa 94558
255-5862
luna@hooked.net
www.lunavineyards.com

MADRIGAL VINEYARDS
3718 St. Helena Highway
Calistoga 94515
942-6577

MARKHAM VINEYARDS
2812 St. Helena Highway North
St. Helena 94574
963-5292
www.markhamvineyards.com

MARSTON VINEYARDS
3600 White Sulphur
Springs Road
St. Helena 94574
963-5069

LOUIS M. MARTINI
   WINERY
254 St. Helena Highway
St. Helena 94574
963-2736
www.louismartini.com

MAYACAMAS VINEYARDS
1155 Lokoya Road
Napa 94558
224-4030
mayacama@napanet.net

McKENZIE-MUELLER
   VINEYARDS
2350 Las Amigas Road
Napa 94558
252-0186

MENDELSON VINEYARD
1226 Third Street
Napa 94559
255-7825

MERRYVALE VINEYARDS
1000 Main Street
St. Helena 94574
963-2225
www.merryvale.com

PETER MICHAEL WINERY
12400 Ida Clayton Road
Calistoga 94515
942-4459
www.petermichaelwinery.com

MILAT VINEYARDS WINERY
1091 St. Helena Highway South
St. Helena 94574
963-0758
info@milat.com
www.milat.com

MINER FAMILY VINEYARDS
7850 Silverado Trail
Oakville 94562
944-9500
www.minerwines.com

ROBERT MONDAVI WINERY
7801 St. Helena Highway
Oakville 94562
963-9611
info@robertmondavi.com
www.robertmondaviwinery.com

MONT ST. JOHN CELLARS
5400 Old Sonoma Road
Napa 94559
255-8864

MONTICELLO VINEYARDS
4242 Big Ranch Road
Napa 94558
253-2802
www.monticellovineyards.com

MOSS CREEK WINERY
6015 Steele Canyon Road
Napa 94558
252-1295

MT. VEEDER WINERY
1999 Mount Veeder Road
Napa 94558
224-4039
jpagano@mtveeder.com

MUMM NAPA VALLEY
8445 Silverado Trail
Rutherford 94573
942-3434
concierge@sparkling.com
www.mumm.com

NAPA CELLARS
7481 St. Helena Highway
Oakville 94562
944-2565
www.napacellars.com

NAPA WINE COMPANY
7830 St. Helena Highway
Oakville 94562
944-8669
production@napawineco.com
www.napawineco.com

NEWLAN VINEYARDS
5225 Solano Avenue
Napa 94558
257-2599

NEWTON VINEYARD
2555 Madrona Avenue
St. Helena 94574
963-9000

NEYERS VINEYARDS
P.O. Box 1028
St. Helena 94574
963-8840

NICHELINI WINERY
2970 Sage Canyon Road
St. Helena 94574
963-0717
www.cris.com/-raw39

NIEBAUM-COPPOLA
ESTATE WINERY
1991 St. Helena Highway
Rutherford 94573
968-1100
www.niebaum-coppola.com

OAKFORD VINEYARDS
P.O. Box 410
Oakville 94562
945-0445

OAKVILLE RANCH
VINEYARDS
7850 Silverado Trail
Oakville 94562
944-9500
www.minerwines.com

ONE VINEYARD
AND WINERY
264 Crystal Springs Road North
St. Helena 94574
963-1123
watson@aol.com

OPUS ONE
7900 St. Helena Highway
Oakville 94562
944-9442
www.opusone.com

PAHLMEYER WINERY
P.O. Box 2410
Napa 94558
255-2321
trade@pahlmeyer.com
www.pahlmeyer.com

PARADIGM
683 Dwyer Road
Oakville 94562
944-1683
info@paradigmwinery.com
www.paradigmwinery.com

ROBERT PECOTA WINERY
3299 Bennett Lane
Calistoga 94515
942-6625
pecota@aol.com
www.robertpecotawinery.com

PEJU PROVINCE WINERY
8466 St. Helena Highway
Rutherford 94573
963-3600
hpeju@aol.com
www.peju.com

MARIO PERELLI-MINETTI
WINERY
1443 Silverado Trail
St. Helena 94574
963-8762

JOSEPH PHELPS
VINEYARDS
200 Taplin Road
St. Helena 94574
963-2745
jpvwines@aol.com
www.jpvwines.com

PINA CELLARS
8060 Silverado Trail
Rutherford 94573
944-2229

PINE RIDGE WINERY
5901 Silverado Trail
Napa 94558
253-7500
info@pineridgewine.com

PLAM VINEYARDS
6200 Washington Street
Yountville 94599
944-1102
kplam@plam.com
www.plam.com

PLUMPJACK WINERY
620 Oakville Crossroad
Napa 94558
945-1220

POPE VALLEY WINERY
6613 Pope Valley Road
Pope Valley 94567
965-9463

PRAGER WINERY AND
PORT WORKS
1281 Lewelling Lane
St. Helena 94574
963-3720
www.pragerport.com

PRIDE MOUNTAIN
VINEYARD
4026 Spring Mountain Road
St. Helena 94574
963-4949
pridemtn@aol.com

QUAIL RIDGE WINERY
1055 Atlas Peak Road
Napa 94558
257-1712
rbi@well.com

QUIXOTE WINERY
6126 Silverado Trail
Napa 94558
944-2659
quixotewinery@yahoo.com

RMS VINEYARDS
1250 Cuttings Wharf Road
Napa 94559
253-9055

KENT RASMUSSEN
WINERY
1001 Silverado Trail
St. Helena 94574
963-5667
krwine@aol.com

RAYMOND VINEYARDS
849 Zinfandel Lane
St. Helena 94574
963-3141

REVERIE ON DIAMOND
MOUNTAIN
1520 Diamond Mountain
Road
Calistoga 94515
942-6800
www.reverie@sonic.net

RITCHIE CREEK VINEYARD
4024 Spring Mountain Road
St. Helena 94574
963-4661

ROMBAUER VINEYARDS
3522 Silverado Trail
St. Helena 94574
963-5170
www.rombauervineyards.com

ROUND HILL WINERY
1680 Silverado Trail
Rutherford 94574
963-5251
www.roundhillwines.com

RUDD ESTATE
500 Oakville Crossroad
Oakville 94562
944-8577

RUSTRIDGE VINEYARD
AND WINERY
2910 Lower Chiles Valley Road
St. Helena 94574
965-2871
rustridge@napanet.net
www.rustridge.com

RUTHERFORD GROVE
WINERY
1673 St. Helena Highway
St. Helena
963-0544
www.rutherfordgrove.com

RUTHERFORD HILL
WINERY
200 Rutherford Hill Road
Rutherford 94573
963-1871
info@rutherfordhill.com
www.rutherfordhill.com

SADDLEBACK CELLARS
7802 Money Road
Oakville 94562
944-1305
www.saddlebackcellars.com

SAGE MOUNTAIN
VINEYARDS
315 Franz Valley School Road
Calistoga 94515
942-1238

ST. CLEMENT VINEYARDS
2867 St. Helena Highway North
St. Helena 94574
963-7221
info@stclement.com
www.stclement.com

ST. SUPÉRY VINEYARDS
AND WINERY
8440 St. Helena Highway
Rutherford 94573
963-4507
divinecab@stsupery.com
www.stsupery.com

SAINTSBURY
1500 Los Carneros Avenue
Napa 94599
252-0592

SALVESTRIN VINEYARD
AND WINE COMPANY
397 Main Street
St. Helena 94574
963-5105

SCHRAMSBERG VINEYARDS
1400 Schramsberg Road
Calistoga 94515
942-4558
schramsbrg@aol.com
www.schramsberg.com

SCHUETZ OLES
P.O. Box 834
St. Helena 94574
963-5121
rschuetz@aol.com

SCHWEIGER VINEYARDS &
WINERY
4015 Spring Mountain Road
St. Helena 94574
963-4882
sally@schweigervineyards.com
www.schweigervineyards.com

SCREAMING EAGLE WINERY
7557 Silverado Trail
Napa 94558
Fax: 944-9271

SEAVEY VINEYARDS
1510 Conn Valley Road
St. Helena 94574
963-8339

SELENE WINES
4101 Big Ranch Road
Napa 94558
258-8119
mia@selenewines.com
www.selenewines.com

SEQUOIA GROVE
VINEYARDS
8338 St. Helena Highway
Rutherford 94573
944-2946
info@sequoiagrove.com
www.sequoiagrove.com

SHAFER VINEYARDS
6154 Silverado Trail
Napa 94558
944-2877
shafer@shafervineyards.com
www.shafervineyards.com

SHOWKET-AWNI WINES
7778 Silverado Trail
Oakville 94562
944-9553
Dorothy@showketvineyards.com
www.showketvineyards.com

SHYPOKE VINEYARD
4170 St. Helena Highway North
Calistoga 94515
942-0420
ggheitz@aol.com

SIGNORELLO VINEYARDS
4500 Silverado Trail
Napa 94558
255-5990

SILVER OAK CELLARS
915 Oakville Crossroad
Oakville 94562
800-273-8809
www.silveroak.com

SILVERADO HILL
CELLARS
3103 Silverado Trail
Napa 94558
253-9306

SILVERADO VINEYARDS
6121 Silverado Trail
Napa 94558
257-1770
info@silveradovineyards.com
www.silveradovineyards.com

ROBERT SINSKEY
VINEYARDS
6320 Silverado Trail
Napa 94558
944-9090
RSV@robertsinskey.com
www.robertsinskey.com

SKY VINEYARDS
1500 Lokoya Drive
Napa 94558
935-1391

SMITH-MADRONE
VINEYARDS
4022 Spring Mountain Road
St. Helena 94574
963-2283

SODA CANYON VINEYARDS
4120 Silverado Trail
Napa 94558

SPARROW LANE
1445 Summit Lake Drive
Angwin 94506
965-9130

SPELLETICH CELLARS
195 Edgewood Place
Angwin 94506
965-0952
spell@fcs.net
www.spellwine.com

SPOTTSWOODE WINERY
1401 Hudson Avenue
St. Helena 94574
963-0134
spottswde@aol.com
www.spottswoode.com

SPRING MOUNTAIN
VINEYARDS
2805 Spring Mountain Road
St. Helena 94574
967-4188

STAGLIN FAMILY VINEYARDS
1570 Bella Oaks Lane
Rutherford 94573
963-1749
info@staglinfamily.com
www.staglinfamily.com

STAG'S LEAP WINE
CELLARS
5766 Silverado Trail
Napa 94558
944-2020
slwc@cask23.com
www.stagsleapwinecellars.com

STAGS' LEAP WINERY
6150 Silverado Trail
Napa 94558
944-1303
www.stagsleapwinery.com

STAR HILL WINERY
1075 Shadybrook Lane
Napa 94558
255-1957

STELTZNER VINEYARDS
5998 Silverado Trail
Napa 94558
252-7272
www.steltzner.com

STERLING VINEYARDS
1111 Dunaweal Lane
Calistoga 94515
942-3344
www.sterlingvineyards.com

STONEGATE WINERY
1183 Dunaweal Lane
Calistoga 94515
942-6500
sgnapa@aol.com

STONEY SPRINGS WINERY
264 Crystal Springs Road
St. Helena 94574
963-7760
cook@napanet.net
www.stoneysprings.com

STONY HILL VINEYARD
P.O. Box 308
St. Helena 94574
963-2636

STORYBOOK MOUNTAIN
3835 Highway 128
Calistoga 94515
942-5310
sigstory@aol.com
www.storybook.wines

SULLIVAN VINEYARDS
1090 Galleron Lane
Rutherford 94573
963-9646
jandj@sullivanwine.com
www.sullivan.com

SUMMIT LAKE VINEYARDS
2000 Summit Lake Drive
Angwin 94508
965-2488
summitlake@summitlake
vineyards.com

SUTTER HOME WINERY
277 St. Helena Highway
St. Helena 94574
963-3104
info@sutterhome.com
www.sutterhome.com

SWANSON VINEYARDS
AND WINERY
1271 Manley Lane
Rutherford 94573
944-0905
www.swansonwines.com

THE TERRACES
P.O. Box 511
Rutherford 94573
963-1707

PHILIP TOGNI VINEYARD
3780 Spring Mountain Road
St. Helena 94574
963-3731

TREFETHEN VINEYARDS
1160 Oak Knoll Avenue
Napa 94558
255-7700
winery@trefethen.com
www.trefethen.com

M. TRINCHERO
FAMILY ESTATE
100 St. Helena Highway South
St. Helena 94574
963-3104
info@sutterhome.com
www.sutterhome.com

TRUCHARD VINEYARDS
3234 Old Sonoma Road
Napa 94559
253-7153

TUDAL WINERY
1015 Big Tree Road
St. Helena 94574
963-3947

TULOCAY WINERY
1426 Coombsville Road
Napa 94559
255-4064

TURLEY WINE CELLARS
3358 St. Helena Highway
St. Helena 94574
963-0940

TURNBULL WINE
CELLARS
8210 St. Helena Highway
Oakville 94562
963-5839
www.turnbullwines.com

V. SATTUI WINERY
1111 White Lane
St. Helena 94574
963-7774
info@vsattui.com
www.vsattui.com

VANDERHEYDEN
VINEYARDS WINERY
4057 Silverado Trail
Napa 94558
257-0130
vvwines@napanet.net

VIADER VINEYARDS INC.
1120 Deer Park Road
St. Helena 94574
963-3816
deliavia@aol.com

VIGIL VINEYARD WINERY
3340 Highway 128
Calistoga 94515
942-2900
vigilwine@aol.com

VILLA ANDRIANA/
SUMMERS WINERY
1172 Tubbs Lane
Calistoga 94515
942-5508
sumranch@aol.com
www.sumwines.com

VILLA HELENA WINERY
1455 Inglewood Avenue
St. Helena 94574
963-4334
vintner@pobox.com

VILLA MT. EDEN WINERY
620 Oakville Crossroad
Oakville 94562
944-2414

VINE CLIFF WINERY
7400 Silverado Trail
Napa 94558
944-1364
info@vinecliff.com
www.vinecliff.com

VOLKER EISELE
FAMILY ESTATE
3080 Lower Chiles Valley Road
St. Helena 94574
965-2260

VON STRASSER WINERY
1510 Diamond Mountain Road
Calistoga 94515
942-0930

WERMUTH WINERY
3942 Silverado Trail
Calistoga 94515
942-5924

WHITE ROCK VINEYARDS
1115 Loma Vista Drive
Napa 94558
257-7922

WHITEHALL LANE
WINERY
1563 St. Helena Highway
St. Helena 94574
963-9454
whthal@aol.com

WHITFORD CELLARS
4047 East Third Avenue
Napa 94558
942-0840

ZD WINES
8383 Silverado Trail
Napa 94558
963-5188
info@zdwines.com

INDEX